It's A Long Story

A First-Person Urban Adventure

— By James Casimir Wisniewski

ISBN: 1-4033-9521-7 (e-book)
ISBN: 1-4033-9522-5 (Paperback)

Library of Congress Control Number: 2002095797

This book is printed on acid free paper.

Printed in the United States of America
Bloomington, IN

1stBooks – rev. 04/23/03

For Alma and Elaine, for believing

We shall not cease from exploration
And the end of all our exploring
Will be to arrive where we started
And know the place for the first time.

— T.S. Eliot,
Four Quartets, "Little Gadding"

Be kind, for everyone you meet
is engaged in a great battle.
— Philo of Alexandria

CONTENTS

"Based on a true story...."

This happened.

It happened when I was age twenty-two. It has been on my mind every day for over thirty years since. I think — I know — that nothing nearly like it has ever happened to anyone else anywhere anytime.

Yeah, right.

I do not reasonably expect that you will believe this. Incredulity is understood, and thus far nearly unanimous among those few who have heard the story. They would like to ascribe it to psychedelics, or self-delusion, or a classic psychotic break.

You figure it out. Pleasant, nostalgic, amusing, innocuous memoir. Until like page 10. Or 63. Try suspending your disbelief beyond that. After page 69, you're on your own.

Go on. Skip ahead if you want to.

By then you may start to see why it took me so long to determine to tell this. The story sounds — *is* — improbable, inexplicable, implausible. And that is the integral essential catch: if no one believes it happened, then of course it didn't, couldn't have happened.

Stranger things have happened. So did this. That is a known fact, not only to me but to others then, and now to you, if you take it as such.

Up to you. Make it easy on yourself: read this as a novel, although the only fiction I have ever written is advertising. Read it as first-personal history and you may then imagine what it has meant to this person.

That's what I want to find out. I cannot, literally for the life of me, not after year after year of daily consideration, figure out any reason why, nor any way how.

Maybe I can find or someone can offer an explanation, although sometimes I think, melodramatically, that this may be vouchsafed to me only at or after the end of this life. I would like to understand better and sooner.

All I can do is put it down. I am working from near-total-recall memory, good sets of notes assembled over the years, and some original documents. The characters and events depicted here are factual. Any similarity to persons living or dead is remarkable. No names have been changed. All trademarks are the property of their respective owners. A decent interval has passed. The statutes of limitations have expired. This is being written for the record and for the writer.

Fair warning: people say they have had nightmares after reading this.

***

First let me cross my blocks

⊠ **Winter, 1970-1971.**
I was 22, living a lifelong (since high school) dream, having the time of my life writing copy for a big consumer ad agency in a gold anodized boxy office building on Portnoy's Corner,

⊠ **E. 51st and Lexington Avenue, New York City 10022,**
diagonally across from the lightning-bolted, deco-gargoyled brick GE HQ, up from the aqua mundane Summit Hotel, across from a newly poured concrete eggcrate containing Arthur Goldberg's law office…my window facing north over cityscape generic except for an iron arch of the 59th Street Bridge, a black-glazed innominate slab, and a sweep of the curtainwall of the Seagram Building, my sundial in spring and fall, shadowed by the advancing afternoons that led me walking crosstown to catch the train up to

⊠ **W. 125th and Broadway, New York City 10027**
where the 7th Avenue IRT subway straddles the intersection like a dinosaur skeleton, at the base of a humped, uphill, Belgian block-paved, dead-end street, where I lived in a $108.91/mo. rent-controlled 1brm., alcove kitch., poster-papered, sidewalk-scavenged semi-furn. apt. — top floor, 6-brick, airshft./crtyd/ fire escp. vu, but from the roof, a vista of statements rising: up the block, the columned cupola of Grant's Tomb; further down, the 30-story spire of Riverside Church; the Jewish and Union Theological Seminaries separated by Broadway; east, the massed high-rise Grant Houses, constellations in their windows at Christmas; west, the mile-wide Hudson River, the staunch hunched Palisades, and across the horizon the silken tensile steel George Washington Bridge.

***

3

Sheer coincidence,

nothing more, at least to start. Just some happenstances:

• The Old Man perforated an ulcer that Christmas, so when I came home to Pittsburgh on the bus I delivered a custom get-well card — 6 or 8 30" x 40" panels with copy on jumbo photostats, featuring a whimsical anatomical Blechmanish cartoon stomach with Band-Aid® (caption: "In the holiday spirit, don't get an ulcer. Give one."), plus a replica, blown up from *Reader's Digest,* of the humanist homily of that epoch, widely reprinted, even recorded, *recitative,* as a soothing pop single — "Desiderata," by one Max Ehrmann (d. 1945):

> *Go placidly amid the noise & haste, & remember what peace there may be in silence. As far as possible without surrender, be on good terms with all people.... You are a child of the universe, no less than the trees & the stars. You have a right to be here. And whether or not it is clear to you, no doubt the universe is unfolding as it should. Therefore be at peace with God, whatever you conceive Him to be, and whatever your labors & aspirations, in the noisy confusion of life, keep peace with your soul. With all its sham, drudgery, & broken dreams, it is still a beautiful world. Be careful. Strive to be happy.*

(No wonder that this inspired a recorded parody, "Deteriorata.")

During the Christmas Eve hospital visit, after the card was splayed to its full length, "Desiderata" came over the bedside radio.

• Mike the Mailman, over beers and cigarettes at the compulsory "We should get together more than once a year" family holiday congregation and ethnic food cornucopia, let me in on a little known crime-fighting tactic. If I ever think someone is about to mug me or pick my pocket, I should just drop my wallet and keys into the nearest mailbox. Never thought of that, I said. Safest place in the city, he said. Then of course he had to tell me about his U.S. Post Office: 600,000 employees...branching to every place worth the name... world's largest fleet of civilian vehicles ...lowest rates in the free world... thousands of miles for a 6¢ stamp ...umpty jillion pieces of mail, 98 or 99 per cent delivered accurately and expeditiously. The letter that took a week to get across town? Just seemed that long.

Maybe a week from sender to receiver, but any delay was likely created before it got into the system or after it got out. Statistics proved it. And when the letter carriers went on strike last summer, you saw what a great job the National Guard did. Didn't know the scheme. Can't throw the mail with bayonets. Maybe now people won't take the service for granted. Of course, Mike walked three blocks to work and finished his route in time to go home for lunch, and the mail went through, even plain-brown-wrappered *Penthouse* and *Playboy*, though he'd heard of the occasional copy getting lost, but those guys, and they knew who they were, were taking an awful big chance with their jobs and pensions just to peek at dirty pictures, which he didn't much care for himself, particularly, and which they wouldn't need if they had a good home life in the first place, and they probably weren't allowed to subscribe anyway. Afterward, the last word of the evening was a call from Aunt Helen, Mike's mother-in-law, warning about the take-home (or else) festive food: Don't eat the *gołąbki.* * People are getting sick.

• Post Office TV spot: popons, cards and packages, jingle up — the old spiritual:

> *Go where I send thee. How shall I send thee?*
> *I'm gonna send thee one by one,*
> *One for the little bitty baby*
> *who was born, born, born in Bethlehem.*
> *Go where I send thee. How shall I send thee?*
> *I'm gonna send thee two by two, two for Paul and Silas,*
> *One for the little bitty baby….*

(Much better than the usual "Mail early" PSAs…and they're running it *at* Christmas. Nice warm timely institutional fulfillment message.)

• Even with my remaining return round-trip ticket, eight or ten hours by Greyhound over the PA and Jersey Turnpikes back to the Port

---

* **gołąbki** (ga woomp' kee or ha loop' kee), *n. (Polish).* Overcooked cabbage roll containing bland mixture of nondescript meat and mealy rice, questionably edible. Also **pigs in blankets, Polish hand grenades.**

Authority Bus Terminal (commonly, aptly called "the Port of Authority"), the way back was going to be a drag, twin-dieseling through brown and black nowhere interrupted by wakeup glaring two-lane tunnels, relieved by a Saran®-wrapped overpriced sandwich of dull day-old some-such at the Post House, Breezewood, PA, "Town of Motels," and naps and smokes and time checks first hopeful then futile, until the long NYC approach — turning the corner from the Walt Whitman Bridge into Jersey, on toward the Joyce Kilmer rest stop, thence through fog and flats to see the mast and floodlit topmost of the Empire State Building away off, at last a hard right revealing the City rising in shining glory above the entrance to the Lincoln Tunnel. A full working night of highway and headlights in a perpetual procession that persisted hours later in my closed eyes.

Much easier — and still, for me, a novelty — to fly, although the only convenient (or available) flight was via TWA to JFK. In PIT in the waiting room, construction and plywood around the Jetway blocked any view of the airplane parked at the gate. Boarding, once out on the apron, I saw a long swept left wing with Nos.1 and 2 engines. Wow. A B707. My first ride on a 707. TWA Ambassador Service, and pretty nearly private: just 4 or 5 other passengers in this posh tube hissing through the night. At JFK the Saarinen terminal, another novelty to me, had looked cleaner and brighter in pictures. 747s, which I had seen only in pictures and once as an empennage protruding outsized from a hangar, appeared downright fat. Back home uptown, I smoke a pipe and drink a Bud and listen to Jose Feliciano, *"Feliz Navidad,"* and George Harrison, "My Sweet Lord," on the radio.

• Elevator door opens, two guys preceded by one big knife get in. "We don't want to hurt you. We're dope fiends. We just want your money."

<<DOPE FIENDS?>>

"Thass OK. I understand. But all I got is three bucks. See? Just bought beer at the *bodega* and this all I got."

"We can't take your three dollars."

"Go ahead. You need it more than I do. I understand. My brother's a dope fiend...just got outta Lexington."

"I just got outta Lexington."

"Take the $3. I'm supposed to get paid tomorrow."

"Forget it. Keep it. We don't *want* your $3. Whadda we gonna do with $3?"

"Hey man, best I can do. You gotta take somethin' for your trouble. C'mon. Jeez."

"Jeez. Alright. We'll take $2…you keep $1."

"OK."

"Take your glasses off."

<<WHAT FOR?>>

"Never saw you guys."

"Take them off anyway. And we're gonna check your I.D. Make sure we got the right person."

<<WHA?>>

(Only other time I got mugged, surrounded and wrapped up by a buncha kids with a screwdriver in a walled-in blind spot below Juilliard, they said they needed to check my I.D. too.)

"Here's your wallet back."

"Can you gimme my glasses back so I can see?"

"Here."

"Never saw ya."

Putting on the glasses, dropped the bag with the 6-pack (I think they nudged it) and as I gathered it up they were gone.

<<GASP>>

It took what seemed 10 or 15 minutes to brake the pulse, damp the shakes, force the breath, call the cops.

"2-6th Precinct, Officer McGarble."

"Wanna report a mugging in the elevator at 4-5 Tiemann Place."

"GUNS OR KNIVES?"

"Big knife. Bowie knife. Biggest knife I ever saw."

"How many and what did they look like?"

"Best dressed muggers I ever saw. Black guy in camel's hair coat, suit and striped tie. Spanish guy, nice grey suede jacket and matching cap. Real polite. They said they were dope fiends."

"Which way'd they go?"

"Dunno. Out of the elevator onna 3rd floor."

"When did this happen?"

"Maybe about 10 or 15 minutes ago."

"Why are you calling *now*?"

"Took me this long to get to a phone."

"Look, all I can do is send a radio car, and they gotta be long gone by now. How much did they get?"

"All I had on me was $3. They only took $2."

"$2? Nothing else? No credit cards, no watch?"

"Don't have any credit cards, and they musta missed my watch." (My Christmas present stainless Timex and, jeez, my Senior Society of 1848 gold and blue enamel chevroned pinky ring.)

"So all they got was $2? You're calling about *$2*?"

"Officer, I just got mugged at knifepoint, OK? I'm not supposed to report that?"

"Awright. Have you seen them before?"

"Yeah. I think they followed me from the *bodega*. I think I've seen them around 125th and Broadway."

"So they might be locals. Would you recognize them if you saw them again?"

"Yeah. Absolutely."

"Well, if you want to look at some pictures, come on over and ask to see the detectives."

"You folks open in the evenings?"

"All night, all day, 24 hours a day, every day. Anytime you wanna come over. Just lemme make sure I understand: you had $3, they took $2?"

"First they didn't want the $3. Then they took two and gave me back one."

"Muggers giving back money. OK. Just wanted to be sure. Said they were *dope fiends*?"

"Uh-huh. Dope fiends. Sounded anachronistic to me too."

"Guess so."

The next morning, Alex the Porter was collecting the bags of trash outside each door along the hall. "Uh, Alex, 'scuse me, but the people who lived here before told me that Alex isn't as dumb as he looks, and he has, uh, friends, and he knows everything that, uh, goes on around here. I think I met a couple of your, y'know, *friends* last night. In the elevator. I think they mighta been disappointed. Maybe this'll square things. Little late, but Merry Christmas."

I handed him a hat — a $20 bill, so called because that's what you put in an officer's hat when he held it out for a gratuity — $20 stuck in an engraved Agency Monarch envelope sealed with three conjoined symbols — hand injecting arm in an Ω-shaped drug program graphic... a symbol.... and either a subway token or "LEXINGTON" in a circle — pencilled over the flap.

"Just call off the dogs, willya, Alex?"

"I understand."

On the brass elevator button plate that night there was a neatly drawn

right under the deep debossed brand name "ARMOR." Alex was the man who polished the armor in the hall. The next night, the peace symbol again, drawn bolder. So I went out for beer to *Las Antillanas* on Broadway, super*bodega* — actual aisles, displays, little shopping carts, checkout counters, products available in more than one brand, with more than one item on the shelf, meat (USDA Commercial) wrapped in plastic packages, almost-new promo posters, shelf talkers, danglers — different place from the last Bud buy, not because I was afraid of a remugging, but one likes to spread one's trade around the neighborhood, and perish forbid that any shopkeeper would get the idea that I bought beer frequently.

As I headed down the street, there was Alex heading back up with a 6-pack-shaped bag. I half-nodded, he half-nodded back. All of a sudden on that whole block of Broadway every neon sign hanging in and over every storefront just lit up all at once. Wow. At the drop of a hat

Coincidences. Curiosities. Happenstances. That's all.

Then things started getting strange. But first...

***

Sesame seedy

The actual, original, prototypical Sesame Street®. I could have tripped over it without knowing.

That summer I moved 15 blocks straight uptown out of my $22-a-week single-room-occupancy "hotel" flop. No more sharing two bathrooms and a communal kitchen with nine (count 'em — 9) other people — Dominican family, Korean girl, Puerto Rican family, plug-ugly old West Side woman, *todo el mundo* Hispanic guy. No more eating off the dresser or peeing in the sink, no more weekly change of cheesecloth linens and lint-trap towels, no more sitting in one chair and looking out one window at an all-night fruit market, no more living every day all year in one room.

One Saturday morning I awoke to some kind of thumping outside, tied on the bathrobe, jammed on my glasses and went to the door just as it was kicked wide open by a fella on his back in the hallway with both feet up in the air. Another morning, I went into the bathroom and heard skittering behind the shower curtain. Little rat trying to climb up out of the tub. So I stuck the stopper in the drain and turned on the shower full blast hot. As the tub filled, the rat swam, so I kept driving it under with the shower spray, but it took a damned disgustingly long time to die. Once I plopped some books on a chair and out of the upholstery plodded a big fat beetle the size of my fist. And every day, roaches, stenches, rubbish, grime all over, with potential instant bummers from any of maybe a thousand other tragicomic tenants.

So what did I expect for 22 bucks a week, (plus $2 weekly "hotel" occupancy tax, refundable after a stay of 4 weeks? "The College Residence Hotel." Were they gonna put "SRO" on the awning?) When I moved out of the University, this was all that was open on short notice in the neighborhood, all I needed for the time being, and in fact more spacious, more private, even, indeed, more *adult* than a 10' x 14' bunkbed double dorm room. But people should not have to live like this. This was not how I envisioned living, even if I had to, and I didn't have to, I eventually convinced myself.)

Albeit uptown, the new place was a complete apartment — three rooms, if the bathroom counted, 3½ rooms with the kitchen. It had been home, such as it was, for Kirk J. Bachler, gangly, rambly

Sinophile and tea snob who was headed to Hong Kong for the summer, and Jan W. Steenblick, John Denver-lookalike pre-medical anthropologist bound for a dig in Alaska.

So as to get me domiciled without losing the lease and consequently the artificially affordable, unfairly economical, lifetime-guarantee inalterable *prix fixe* rent control, we arranged a pseudo-sublet, telling the Bella the Landlord, a name uttered through clenched teeth in contemptuous undertone (not unusual for landlords anywhere), that I was just watching over the place for the summer while Jan (Bella pronounced his last name "Steinblick," thought he was Jewish, liked him) stayed at the bedside of his allegedly very sick father in Florida.

And so one Saturday night in June I loaded my stuff into a green VW Beetle driven by Old Mark Ryan, kid art director and sidekick, who lived with his family in White Plains and dug coming in to the city for weekend adventures. Two trips. Old Mark no sooner saw not even the apartment but just the lobby, elevator, and 6th floor hall and said "Wisniewski, you just moved from one slum into a bigger one."

(Nonetheless: one morning that fall, split a cab to work with Fiore, kid writer who lived somewhere Villagey but last night had crashed uptown and showed up walking down my block. He mentioned that a friend of his lived in a luxury housing development in the neighborhood. I allowed as to how, unless he meant one of the grand addresses on Riverside Drive, most any housing was a luxury up here.)

As I was settling in, Kirk was still packing his bindlestiff for the Crown Colony and hanging out with his girlfriend, the pneumatically endowed and auspiciously named Leslee Smoke, bunking in the living room on Kirk's bed, plywood platform covered with a carpet remnant. From there they were fixated on my 14" black-and-white Panasonic® TV, a real novelty; for most folky folk then, watching much less owning a TV was *infra dig*. "We were watching 'Sesame Street,' and it was really interesting."

Of course. We all had our childlike moments, them especially. Never ever saw the show myself, although it was brand-new, instantly renowned, reputedly revolutionary, but I could only catch kiddie TV on Saturday mornings.

The show came up again months later as Vinnie ("the Art Director" almost goes without saying, as half the people in that trade must be named "Vinnie") Gatto and I were working on a series of TV spots introducing new brands of cookies. At least the cookie containers were new, designed to convert to hand puppets — grinny monster Gronks™ and march-of-the-cardboard-soldiers Bandsmen boxes with biscuits patterned after the packages and baked according to an Animal Crackerish recipe.

It wasn't long before Vinnie segued into his Cookie Monster™ impression, and I did my impression of his, with tone and accent ultimately much closer to the real McCookie, who has always seemed to me to be part Polish. Thence Vinnie explained to me all about Sesame Street, the application of advertising techniques and stylized animation as teaching tools, and the compelling interest it held not only for his kids but for him. I observed that this might be the best way yet to teach art directors how to read and write. "You'll be able to figure out the little black marks under the pictures. But hey, I know you guys work hard. You must get tired moving your lips when you read. Can you say 'dyslexia'? I knew you could. Besides, you set a good example for your sons: when you color, you stay inside the lines. Hey, I kid art directors — because I don't have to be one."

(Art directors could kid back. Once for whatever reason we mummified Vinnie's phone in masking tape. Next day I came in to find my office door taped hermetically shut, and no one would lend me an X-Acto® knife. Another time I closed my door, which was interpreted as an anti-social gesture by the peripatetic bull session outside. Emerging, I found a foot-high, highly detailed color rendering of a prick stuck under my nameplate.)

I wondered aloud about doing kids' cookie commercials *à la* Sesame Street: in advertising, derivative is original. Maybe a character endorsement, with community-spirited child-oriented benevolent sponsorship ruboff value. Not a good idea, Vinnie said: they're copyrighted and trademarked all over, and PBS *is*, after all, non-commercial. But we did "Gronk-Gronk, Cookie, Cookie" at each other often enough that I got the material for a plausible Sesame facsimile.

Then I discovered the genuine article. One night I was sharing some Schaefer's with a 6th floor neighbor, a Mizz Ada Irene Swazey,

86-year old retired Army nurse, Canadian émigré, veteran of the Harvard Regiment in WWI, who usually sat in the chair across from the gilt plaster lions in the lobby and scooted across to the *bodega* each evening with her dog Skippy to get her rations: one can of Alpo® dog food, two cans of Schaefer beer ("The one beer to have when you're having more than one.") Quite a character, Mizz Swazey was.

Waitaminnit. Something curious and coincidental about not only that character but this very address. Now I recall....

Sesame Street started as a real place. The physical, geographical inspiration, as I remembered from a newsmagazine story, was a New York City block with paving stones stuck in it like sesame seeds on a bun...a street that sloped, dipped, rose, and pitched so that even the cop cars had to slow down...a place where on Sundays, all the kids came out and played on the sidewalk...home to a lotta people...a teemin' place...*Tiemann** Place. Right here, right where I lived, where the originators themselves presumably lived, right along with the characters who animated the original imaginary block. From some TV clips or illustrations I recalled the cartoons and recognized their human models:

☞ Woman in a red and blue nurse's uniform who skittered across the street with two dogs wearing Red Cross insignia blankets: the Nice Nurse, none other than Mizz Ada Irene Swazey herself.

(Himself, as it turned out. Swazey had a man's hands, forearms, and Adam's apple, and was in fact a 54-year old blind disabled cop in old lady drag with a terrier seeing-eye dog. Why he chose to live in that style I'll never know, but I guess he got away with it.)

☞ Fella in a brown fedora and sportcoat who popped out to give the sidewalk a few swift sweeps and popped back in again: Alex the Porter.

☞ Stout sphere-faced man in a racing cap who stood on the stoop with his arms folded across his belly: Mr. Miller the Super.

---

* Named after Mayor Daniel Tiemann (1858-1860); street often confused with Tremont Ave. in the Bronx, which may or may not be paved with Belgian block, like half the streets in Pittsburgh used to be, so the model could have been anyplace, not necessarily Tiemann. Hey, what do I know? Anyway, I now live in what was Mr. Rogers' Neighborhood.

☞ Skinny bespectacled guy who flung open his window and hollered at the sound of breaking glass: Davis from Downstairs, the courtyard music volume control and burglar alarm.

☞ Soprano scales shrilling up the airshaft: Miss Kennard, the Juilliard teacher from across the hall.

☞ Flock of pigeons rising in a fluttering rush: old woman all in black who fed the birds at the foot of the steps leading up to the margin of Riverside Park.

☞ Street saxophonist: the short-order cook from the corner drugstore who used his breaks to blow his horn at the corner of Tiemann and Broadway.

O my. This must be the place. Who knew? Here I am living right on Sesame Street. I have an apartment in a TV show. Wait'll I tell Vinnie. Which I did, but he told his *paisan* Charlie Bellante the TV producer, who did his Groucho shuffle into my office, puffed a pungent cloud out of his Parodi, raised his eyebrows and shook his head at me. "Jeez, Charlie. I didn't know. I had no idea. Never even saw the show. Old Mark helped me move and he said I was just moving from one slum into another. Fiore said something about a friend in a luxury housing development. Jeez, Charlie. Hey, anybody asks me, I don't know from nuttin'."

<<I AM LIVING IN BRIGADOON.
I AM SITTING ON A DIAMOND AS BIG AS THE RITZ.>>

***

The Boy in the Gray Flannel Suit

Tweed Middishade® high school graduation suit, actually, since I got the job at 19, directly from college dropout to youngest copywriter in the business — too ingenuous to be intimidated or even impressed either with myself or my surroundings.

Besides, these were heady days. Uncannily I found myself in the rightest place at the rightest time, with revolutions rolling all around, from the masses to the media, from the streets straight up to the executive suites. 1968 resonated with 1848, with '68 reverbs 20, 25, and 30 years thereafter in magazine commemorative issues and documentary retrospectives. These are the definitive Nielsen diaries of that day. The whole world *was* watching.

Advertising — the art of changing people's minds — was changing itself radically. Mind-altering, -expanding, -affirming, opening with VW, Avis, and the LBJ "Daisy" campaign spot, and leading to Benson & Hedges to Braniff and beyond, the creative revolution was now in full torque — sensibilities, strategies, styles, sans serif type, all new and improved. Baby boomers were massing into markets. Youth would be served, though sometimes not well: "Wow! KENT® got it all together!" ..."Long live The Dry Look®"... "Up With People!" ... Pan Am's first 747, the Clipper "Young America" ... "Ultra Brite® gives your mouth sex appeal" ... Tijuana Smalls™ Little Cigars...not to mention endless shameless ripoffs of *Hair*, hobbits, Hashbury, and other psychedelicacies from Carnaby Street to cryptype concert posters. Even the squarest ad shops wanted to be at least a little hip. The middle-American middle-of-the-road came upon a midlife crisis. The three-martini lunchees met the hash brownie munchies. It was a very good time to be young.

Talk about lucking out. This was what I had always wanted to do — "always" measured as the three or four years in which my mind had been made up.

It had not been a difficult decision. There was no full-body-cavity soul-searching. Most options ruled themselves out readily. Early on, the Old Man (not to mention my Little League coach, wood shop teacher, and many arts and crafts counselors) recognized that I had the dexterity, coordination, and fine motor skills of a manic klutz. That eliminated dentistry: the Old Man was a little disappointed that I

15

would not be able to hang my shingle under his, but not I, not in the least. He had his office in the front of the house, with the family residing behind and above; on Saturday mornings when I was growing up, the school kids had their appointments, so as I settled down to a brunch of Cocoa Puffs® and cartoons, through the halls and up the furnace vents came the sounds of children whining and hollering in supplication and dread. "Jeez, Stanley, I haven't touched you yet; c'mon, open up. This isn't gonna hurt." Thence formed an impression that my father was a man all in white who instilled terror in children. Further deterrent: patients who called Saturday or Sunday afternoon with an abscess they had been nursing for a week, or a plate that had been broken for a month.

Not that I had many other role models. The only other professionals in our blue-collar ethnic neighborhood were a couple of G.P.s, a pharmacist, and another dentist, a Polish D.P.* who presented a certain competitive threat because he administered nitrous oxide. The only white-collar workers were a few men who were shortsleeved, stick-armed eyeshaded bookkeepers or clerks, plus a handful of secretaries and retail salesladies (about as liberated as women got, not that decent women were supposed to have any occupations but homemaker or *bábka*, the latter obliged to attend Mass daily, novenas weekly, funerals regularly, intoning the Polish "*Dobrí Jésù*" recessional in a fingernails-on-blackboard keening screech, *tempo superslomo*.) A "good job" meant working for the city, county, or state, although the payrollers didn't really seem to work much, even the police. ("What does your dad do for a living?" "Nothing. He's a cop.") Skilled laborers fared well enough between steel strikes and layoffs, but I had enough trouble mastering sweeping and snow-shoveling skills, not to mention snobbery approaching manifest predestiny.

I was good at reading and writing, so I figured I could do something that involved those. The Old Man decided on teaching — even prompted one of his favorite *pro Deo* patients, parochial high school teacher and pederast, to plug the idea when he stayed for dinner after an appointment. "James, you really ought to consider

---

* Displaced Person, euphemism for refugee, as well as expression of disdain; the second generation looked down on the newest arrivals from the Old Country.

teaching. You might very well have a gift for it — on the secondary level or beyond."

"I'm certainly giving it some serious thought." Yeah, right. After dinner:

"He's the last person I'd wanna take advice from."

"What's the matter with you, Jimmy?"

"Do you have any idea about this guy?"

"What?"

"Ask anybody at school about him."

"About what? What's the matter with you?"

"I'll tell you about him sometime."

"Tell me about *what*?"

"Never mind." (Outing that person to the Old Man, not that it would ever have been believed, would have been tantamount to sacrilege, on top of some unspecified perversion on my part.)

Jeez. Open secret, inside info even passed down to eighth-grade prospective freshboys. From students to faculty and administrators, everybody knew, many firsthand; if anyone ever complained, nobody heard and nothing ever happened.

The celibacy and credibility of the spokesman aside, I wasn't about to become a teacher. Same old same old, semester after semester, and not all students were as challenging and rewarding as I was. Besides, how many teachers became famous?

The Old Man did not understand the idea of writing for a living. Not that he wasn't at least a fluent if formal writer himself, trained, we were often reminded, on a Polish typewriter, which would render the usual high school or college paper in an órnãtêlý êmbèllîshéd, êxótîç ãnd èthnîç dìáçrîtíçâl pîdgîn whïçh démónstrâtèd dêtérmínátîòn âš wéll ãš â çèrtàîn bílìnguâl fàçîlíty. Even to me this was impressive, especially considering that his parents neither read nor wrote English or Polish, yet their "X"s stood with full American legal validity when affixed to deeds giving each of their five children their own brick row houses.

Nor did the Old Man understand the idea of writing advertising for a living. That was not just geographical — it came from someplace else, out there, "Madison Avenue" — but generational. Born on the same weekend as the Ed Sullivan show, I grew up to novel admonitions: "Jimmy, don't sit too close to the TV. Jimmy, turn that radio down." Sitting too close, with the volume full blast, I got the messages. I *liked* the commercials. I believed in Colgate's Happy Tooth and Mr. Tooth Decay. I lusted after the Doublemint Twins and Julie London torching "You get a lot to like with a Marlboro: filter, flavor, flip-top box." Along with most of my cohort, I can still replay 40-year-old jingles verbatim. And I knew exactly what writers did: it was just like "The Dick Van Dyke Show." (Of course, my sister enlisted in the U.S. Marine Corps believing that it was just like "Gomer Pyle, U.S.M.C.")

Deep in the background there was an intriguing impression from "Mr. Blandings Builds His Dream House" — beyond the suburban domesticity, which was a foreign country and culture, and the characters, who bore no resemblance to anyone in my neighborhood or knowledge, but Cary Grant's serendipitous discovery of the breakthrough slogan, "Wham™ — The Ham What Am" or words to that effect. Interesting. People actually got paid to do that.

When I saw Volkswagen and Avis ads, I thought, "They're talking to me. I can do that." Then, in the *Atlantic Monthly* I stopped on a black-and-white page headed

If you can write an ad for Olympia typewriters, we'll send you our copywriter's salary for a month —

with a check for like $1250 or $1500[*] cranking out of the carriage of a portable typewriter. Hey! I *could* do that. So I thought. In a little while, I did.

Nineteen-year-olds came cheap then: $6,000 (plus fringes and profit sharing) to start. (As a minor under the protection of the State of New York Department of Labor, I was permitted to work no more than 40 hours per week, documented by weekly vouchers fraudulently executed and signed by myself and my supervisor. Hey, bust me.)

The kid paid his dues writing grocery trade ads, "Brought to you by" lead-ins, live radio ("Flood waters are disease waters. Help protect your family by washing with Lysol Brand Disinfectant"), and

---

[*] The minimum wage was $1.40 then. Cadillacs cost less than $10,000. In college, my tuition was $1900 a year. My faculty adviser, an associate professor, made $9600 a year.

comprehensive packages for the beloved Arthur Godfrey[*], America's greatest salesman. With one of the last live network radio shows, Arthur required detailed product fact sheets and sample scripts, 30-, 60-, and 90-seconds, topped by the omnibus 2-minute *ex tempore spiel,* not easy to fill with the obligatory four or six key copy points, so often embellished with Godfreyisms: "Take it from me," "I really believe in this product," "Y'know, I've used this myself, and I gotta tell you it's special."

Along the way, I learned the craft, OJT, on Lysol® Brand Spray Disinfectant, Deodorizing Cleaner, Toilet Bowl Cleaner, and Basin Tub & Tile Cleaner... Lipton® Main Dishes™ — Beef Stroganoff, Ham Cheddarton, Chicken Primavera, Chicken Supreme with Sherry...Sunshine® Biscuits...Teacher's® Scotch...del Magnifico™ Chianti ...Maryland® Cigarettes... S&H® Green Stamps ..."all®" Detergent with Bleach, Borax, and Brighteners ...Dishwasher "all" ... Pepsodent® Toothpaste...Nytol®... Norwich Pharmacal New Products[**] ...and, as we tend to say in ad copy litany, many, many more.

Every day I got to go to work in my own *wunderkindergarten.* Originally, this was a narrow yellow-metal-and-glass cubicle surrounded by a busy and noisy casting department, the redeeming feature of which was the periodic cattle (or calf) call for the Cover Girl, Noxzema, Arrid, or Breck accounts. Imagine a roundup of the most impressive redheads in the business (including the demi-goddess I casually helped after lunch one day when the receptionist was out, and next saw on the cover of *Cosmo,* the tantalizing J.J. Kinnersley), or a clutch of Cheryl Tiegs or Jaclyn Smith clones, or Diahann Carroll doubles (the only sure bet for minority household roles), or, auditioning for my Lysol Spray room deodorizer spots, a reception room with a pack of bloodhounds.

---

[*] Never met the Ole Redhead in person, but at an agency tour and "creative seminar" at radio station WNEW, encountered Julius LaRosa. This was a big deal to the folks back home, who remembered when Godfrey had summarily fired Julius on the air. *Much* bigger deal: the great DJ William B. Williams himself stuck his head in and complimented me on my pipes.

[**] Including a tushy deodorant spray I suggested naming "Butte" or "Preparation 'O'." I did once balk at an assignment for a feminine hygiene product named "Lysette®."

Shortly thereafter, a real office with walls, ceiling, and door (but no window) opened up. For the column running up right through the middle, I finagled a mockup sign:

This was lost on the Capotean writer in the next-door office (*sans* column cover), but then, everything he wrote rhymed.

After I missed out on a temporary relocation to the Republic of Viet Nam by flunking my draft physical (trigger eye < 20/200, not up to military standards, although I failed to mention that I was a decent, in fact natural shot with a target rifle), I got a raise. Ultimately I got a window and an office worth decorating — scrounged furniture, including the only bookcase on the floor (which nearly got me tapped for the Literary Guild account), filled with a few shelves of hip books, a big plaster No.1, a horseshoe crab, a rubber frog that stuck out its tongue when squeezed, Gronk puppets and other whimsies, plus the obligatory shrine of client products; a wall of pretty fair caricatures of myself, hanging above a jackhammer of an Olympic manual typewriter; an outsize C-print of an illustrated ad hound dog ("Take it from me, the world's most sensitive nose, there's nothing like Lysol Spray for odors and household germs"); a certificate from Daniel Starch & Staff and signed by Leo Burnett himself, citing that ad as one of the 100 Best Read of 1969; a Burnett agency self-promo ad which I had seen and saved back in high school:

(pic: line art — bronze sculpture, hand reaching heavenward, *à la* Burnett corporate logo)

(headline)

When you reach for the stars you may not quite get one, but you won't come up with a handful of mud either.

...plus an NYPD "How to describe a criminal" flyer; posters of Mr. Spock, Middle Earth, *Guernica,* and over the bookcase, King Kong flexing above a sheet metal sign swiped from my apartment building:

DOGS

NOT ALLOWED

ON THIS ROOF

BOARD OF HEALTH

Beneath, a fuzzy throw rug with imitation Disney characters ("A title on the door rates a Bigelow® on the floor.")

At Christmas, when kids came in to see where Dad or Mom worked and then had a festive lunch at The Cattleman, a secretary peeked in with two dressed-up youngsters. "Mr. Weithas's[*] children," she said. "He thought that they should see this."

"Hiya kids. Your dad's office is a lot nicer, but they let us have more fun up here."

***

---

[*] Mr. Weithas, with whom I traded Polish and elephant jokes in the interoffice mail, was a management supervisor who ultimately became chairman of the whole shebang, and in fact of the entire American Association of Advertising Agencies.

Tune in, turn on, sell out

Right before I determined to seek my fortune in advertising, I had planned to enlist in the U.S. Army and become chairman of the Joint Chiefs of Staff. For this I read von Clausewitz, followed the siege of Khe Sanh daily in the *Times*, took long walks through Riverside Park, and began to drink beer.

In retrospect, I was trying to manage one of my first flanking assaults of major depression. In real time, I was looking for an out. Eventually my next-door dorm neighbor, Bob Martin, Navy brat, Young Republican, and hawk, became concerned enough, either about me or the U.S. military, to initiate therapy.

Psychodrama had precedent with us. We had known each other well over a year before Bob divulged that he was gay, this at a time when gay was not at all cool but criminal. Not only that, he was a gay activist and in fact a pioneer of the homophile movement. Bob also occasionally got dressed up in his USN-issue sailor suit ("seafood" ..."Chicken of the Sea") and hustled in Times Square for pocket money.

Ultimately he led me on excursions into his netherworld — my in-depth introduction to that subculture, its characters, costumes, codes, and deep cover. For sociological study, he took me cruising on Christopher Street ("The way that guy leered: does that mean...? Like, he wanted *me?*"), barhopping with the butch set ("I feel so *underleathered*"), and a safari to the Times Square costume show/meat rack ("Now I understand the real meaning of 'trick or treat.'") Through him I met founding fathers (and a mother) of the gay liberation movement, now elder statespeople.

Once, in his 9' x 14' dorm room, he even staged an eight-man orgy for my orientation and edification. That experience demonstrated that sex was sex was sex for any gender, though not necessarily for me. Even with an open "I'll-try-anything-once" mind and a healthy "Hey, why rule out half the population?" curiosity, and notwithstanding the solicitous oral ministrations of several attractive, pleasant, and evidently skilled young men, I turned out to be a complete flop. Performance canceled. No-show. Non-starter.

The one consolation and redeeming social value: the next day, while flattening out his 8" x 10" black-and-white glossy politicianheadshot pinups that had curled in the orgiastic heat and humidity, Bob confided, "We have decided that you are the straightest person we have ever seen."

In the current case, psychopharmacology applied as the therapy of choice. Bob prescribed and administered to me my first dose of lysergic acid diethylamide-25: he gave me a little piece of a tablet, a large crumb, then another crumb, then put the Beatles[*] on his phonograph and watched over me as my psyche went tropic.

"A person is never the same after an acid trip."

"Acid rearranges the pieces on the chessboard of the mind."

"Acid dissolves the glue that holds the self together, and the self may reassemble itself differently."

"Acid is indescribable and individual. You have to do it to know it."

"Acid is unlike any other experience you have ever had."

"Acid produces a psychic orgasm."

"Acid will replace movies and TV."

"Acid will reveal the meaning of life."

"Acid is birth, death, resurrection."

"Acid will give you a glimpse of God."

So I had heard tell. Not quite. None of the above. Acid projected an afternoon's worth of plotless Day-Glo™ cartoons and op art cycloramas inside my eyelids, and amplified individual Beatles' notes and syllables to 3D, 4-color, freeze-frame waveforms breaking along my auditory canals. But no anagnorisis, no epiphany, no revelation, no beatific vision.

The letdown was almost as disappointing as my First Holy Communion, when I earnestly expected to feel a divine presence within, specifically as a luminescent Ben-Gay® warmth upwards in my chest and around my shoulders. Nonetheless, walking across campus through glittering snow to get a post-trip deli snack, I thought about rethinking.

Plan B. The next night, to a small cohort of Marlboro-smoking fellow-travelers and fellow-sufferers, gathered as usual in a dorm lobby hideaway lounge notable for its portrait of Lou Gehrig in a

---

[*] "Magical Mystery Tour," an obvious choice, then "Sergeant Pepper," "Rubber Soul," "Revolver," thence *da capo*.

Columbia uniform, I announced that I was going to go out and get a job in advertising.

This was met with derision. No surprise. The Second Coming would have been met with derision in the Gehrig Room. Nothing was sacred, no one was taken seriously. My announcement produced the expected sarcasms, cynicisms — and one voluntary, unsolicited pledge in writing from a history major generally noted for his serene civility:

If Wizard gets a job in advertising by April 1, 1968, I will personally give him a blow job at the Sundial at high noon.

/s/ R. Wilson

Richard Wilson had probably never even received — much less given — a blow job in his life. I certainly didn't want one from him at the Sundial at the epicenter of campus; better he should have offered just to kiss my ass at high noon. Still, this added an incentive.

***

And so I ventured out, equipped with orange plastic binders of writing samples — a slew of crudely executed speculative ads, and an array of pretty respectable printed samples from the school yearbook and humor magazine. Among the samples, the first ad I ever wrote, a parody of the then-current Berlitz campaign —

Esto es publicidad para Berlitz.

See? You already know some Spanish. And in a matter of weeks you could be speaking it fluently. Because the Berlitz method is the fastest and most effective way to learn any language....

Thence, the *Jester* version:

LBJ is a scum-sucking capitalist pig.

See? You already know some Activist. And in a matter of weeks you could be speaking it fluently.... Just as we did here, you start right in haranguing. Loud. Your instructor won't speak a word of sensible English to you. He starts right out with "Screw you"....

We can have you arguing fluently in five weeks if you're not in jail or in a hyper-bourgeois, or in three or four months if you can only spare a few hours away from draft appeal hearings. (Or in ten to fifteen days, if you refuse to even pay lip service to the running dogs of Wall Street.)

We guarantee our method if you guarantee your soul, baby....

Funny, but nobody in the ad biz who interviewed me seemed to get it. "See, it's not a political statement. It's a *parody*. It's making fun of leftist language."

Out in the realistic world:

"I admire what you're doing, but let me give you some advice: stay in school. Come see us in a year or so."

"I think there's an opening for a proofreader at *American Heritage*. Now, you'd have to take a proofreading test."

"What the heck's going on up at that school of yours?"

"I can't believe Columbia doesn't offer any undergraduate business courses."

"We usually put entry-level people in the mailroom, so they can get a complete overview of the agency's operations."

"I thought most people of your generation held this business in contempt."

"You know that you could get drafted as soon as you leave school. That can make an employer nervous. I guess it might make you nervous too."

"There's nothing open now, but you know how fast this business changes. We may need someone tomorrow."

"If you have to move out of the dorms, you might think of staying at the Y."

"Usually we hire people with around ten years' experience working in other shops."

"Please complete and return the enclosed copy test."

"We will keep your résumé on file should any openings develop."

"You might think about starting in retail."

"James WHO?"

"He's in a meeting."

"He's still in a meeting."

"He'll call you right back."

"James Casimir WHO?"

"Would you spell that, please?"

"And where are you working now?"

"Don't take a mailroom job. After a month you'd start tearing up the mail and throwing it all over the place."

"I'll camp out on his desk and have him call you first thing tomorrow."

"I have this writer here who's all of 19...."

Six weeks after I started looking, I was hired as a copywriter at SSCandB, Inc., the sixth-largest advertising agency in the world.

I rode the Staten Island Ferry back and forth, gaping at Manhattan lighting up in synch with the dusk advancing block upon block. O what a beautiful city. My town. What a day. What a night. What luck. What...destiny. I *knew* it would work out this way. This was straight out of the double-feature movies we used to watch on TV at home on Sundays. This was every cornball kid-from-the-sticks, star-is-born "New York, I'll get you yet" success story ever made, every stock shot skyline ever shown, every cliché I ever believed. It all came true. It had to.

I felt obliged to get a bottle of something to celebrate with, and knowing next to nothing about booze, got a half-gallon jug of 11 Cellars Tawny Port. (Port sounded both strong and statusy, but a mere fifth hardly seemed festive, and nowhere near enough, although the liquor store clerk asked if I planned to use this in some kinda punch.)

Eventually I found myself down deep into the eleventh cellar, lost between my top bunk and the sink, whereupon an emissary from the Gehrig Room came by to confirm that I was all right. Wilson, of all people. He made sure that I was not using the bunk as an ashtray, nor the wastebasket as an emesis basin, nor the window as an exit, then helped me close the port and go down for the count into the bottom bunk. "Hey, Wilson, thanks, man. By the way, I still have that IOU you gave me."

***

Then all 1968 broke loose.

On March 31, the Sunday before my first day on the job, LBJ abdicated. I watched his address in black-and-white in a standing-room-only dormitory TV room. Nobody cheered. Hardly anybody even commented. Nobody seemed to know what to make of it. Did *we* do that? Couldn't be. Did we win? Don't count on it. Was the war about to end? Don't hold your breath. Now what? Your guess is as good as mine. For all we thought we knew, as much as we had continually talked about its inevitability, we could not recognize qualitative change for what it was, even as it stared down at us balefully from the TV and rasped its imminence.

Three days later the Rev. Dr. Martin Luther King Jr. was killed. I heard the news as a light-sleeping dream during an after-work nap with the radio on, and awoke wide to the fact. I thought I had to go someplace and talk to somebody, so I headed up to school. Herman Maisonet, black Puerto Rican pre-med, came into the Gehrig Room from a pass through Harlem and said there were many people coming out and milling around. "Mostly students," he said. Naw. He meant young people, but "student" had become a code word for "partisan." Us (I was still essentially "us") and them. Which side are you on?

That night, Mayor Lindsay went uptown and walked the streets in his shirtsleeves, grieved and worried and cried with everyone else out that night, and that alone may have kept the peace. But the next morning on the subway to work, I thought every black person I saw was staring fists right through me. Still, once I got my morning coffee to go at the Chock Full o' Nuts on our ground floor, I didn't see any more black persons.

Three quotes still come to mind:

> *Shoot to maim looters. Shoot to kill arsonists.*
> -Mayor Richard A. Daley;

> *In New York we do not shoot children.*
> -Mayor John V. Lindsay

James Casimir Wisniewski

And perhaps a year later, at an Agency-wide creative department review and revival meeting,

> We need to get more colored people into our advertising.
>   -Creative Director Richard R. Uhl.

Before I had been on the job a month, Columbia up and took leave of its senses. The first night, just another common ordinary sit-in around the College administration's offices: both the Students' Afro-American Society and Students for a Democratic Society, protesting any one or more of an inexhaustible lode of outrages, vowing not to leave until their demands were met or until hell froze over. Meantime, convened as usual in the Gehrig Room, both the Students for an Apathetic Society ("We do not picket. We loiter.") and the Small Furry Animals were generally snickering ("These people think 'underground' means low budget movies"), and preparing to sell tickets to The Freezing Over of Hell. Then SAS either wanted the issue or the sit-in for themselves, or just some breathing room, so they told the pukes* to leave.

SDS stomped out and meandered around until it could find its very own building to sit in, although absent anyone inside to protest to. The crack University Security Police, consisting of geriatric night watchmen and various stalwarts dubbed "Sergeant Schultz," "Sergeant Garcia," "Depitty Dawg," and "Barney Fife," followed standard procedure and slept. Late. By sometime the next day, scouting parties and splinter groups had occupied maybe a dozen buildings on campus.

"If there's a panty raid at Harvard," a Columbia trustee once groused, "it makes the front page of the *Crimson.* If there's a panty raid at Columbia, it makes the front page of the *Times*" (actually, usually the break page, below the fold.) This made the cover of *LIFE* and then some.

------

* **puke** (py›k) *Slang. n.* A hippie or radical activist. (Mildly pejorative; orig. from "I see these people and they make me want to *puke,*" attrib. to a **jock** (q.v.) Also see **grub, tweed, flame, freak.**)

The media didn't quite know what to make of it. Neither did I, though I was less alarmed or even concerned than perplexed. The news shrilled "Riot!" Hardly, with a pickup grab-bag of non-violent *naïfs* and raving rhetoricians. Nor did I understand what the pukes were calling it. "The strike." *Strike?* I comprehended that in terms of a work stoppage by the United Steelworkers or Mineworkers or Local 249, International Brotherhood of Teamsters, Chauffeurs, Warehousemen, & *Amici Nostri*. But a school stoppage? If you decide not to attend class, even for an entire semester (which I tried in a couple sociology courses and got an A- and a B+), you're not on strike. You're cutting class. If you don't want to study, that's called "fucking off." (Tried that too — worked perfectly: I didn't learn anything.) In any case, stopping education was not analogous to stopping production. This was more like a consumer boycott, except that the consumers had paid in advance. No economic skin off the school's nose. Nonetheless, "Strike!" sounded dramatic and heroic, resonating with the I.W.W., European general strikes, and the noble radical ideal of "building a worker-student alliance." Not that any SDS member ever worked (or wanted) a union job, or hit the bricks on a real picket line, nor that the rank-and-file proletariat felt a whole lot of solidarity with bourgeois Ivy League commie hippie homo peaceniks.

Neither could I figure out what the demonstrators planned to do with the buildings they were occupying — nor, I imagine, could they. Structures do not seem to make very good hostages.[*] A siege mentality is not a siege.

Besides, why here? "But son," the cartoon mom said to the protestor, "this is the college of your *choice*." *Akademiesluft macht frei.* The University extended and protected degrees of freedom — freedom of speech, action, press (or copier or mimeograph), behavior, and *bien être* — largely unavailable in the outside world. If we were free at all, anywhere at all, we were freest here. This was sanctuary, home and hearth. The University was not "them" but "us." Dwight Eisenhower found that out before he moved up to head a younger but

---

[*] Possible precedent: when Columbia owned the land under Rockefeller Center, the University Band played its traditional Christmas concert around the great tree, then marched around with picket signs reading "TAKE YOUR BUILDINGS AND LEAVE."

larger institution. As University president, he began an address to a faculty meeting with "All right now, you employees of Columbia University," whereupon a professor rose in the back of the room and declared "Sir, we *are* Columbia University."

I thought the University could have resolved the issues at hand by owning up to some blunders. It wasn't as if people were demanding a million dollars, a plane to Cuba, and amnesty for the school's political prisoners, much less better food in the dining halls. Nahh. Admitting, let alone correcting mistakes would be too easy. So presently one evening I happened upon a tight caravan of school buses painted green, black, and white, lettered "P O L I C E," crammed with big cops with hats and bats. It had come to this between us, formerly including me, and them, formerly us.

The uprising even did me a bit of good. My mother wrote that the family now felt a little relieved that I had left school because I wouldn't be in the middle of the riots, not that I would have been except as a sidewalk superintendent.

At work I mostly echoed the family sentiment and shook my head a lot in dismay. Still, on the partition outside my cubicle I had to hang the instant black-and-white commemorative poster, bloody-faced kid flashing a peace sign amidst the embattled, headline "HAIL COLUMBIA!", with my caption

LIBERATED ZONE #1

Let us have one, two, many Columbias.
-Che.

Some passersby in the office seemed to disapprove visibly.

✌ Early in the morning of June 5, my 20th birthday, Bobby Kennedy was shot. Migod. They're killing everybody.

[Early in Kennedy's term as the junior senator from New York, the Columbia *Jester* invited him to our homecoming football game against Harvard. Understanding that RFK was new to the area and might be unfamiliar with certain parts of the city, *Jester* considerately included directions — from Boston to New York, into Manhattan, thence to the game at Baker Field, by car, bus, or subway, via detailed and neatly mapped routes with tourist attractions and historical sites highlighted, subway token included. There may have even been a notation about the best place to check his carpetbag. We got back a polite standard letter of thanks and regret from an aide, who added a handwritten line: "P.S. The Senator also wishes me to inform you that he thinks Columbia is a shitty school."]

Robert Kennedy lay in state at St. Patrick's Cathedral, right on the way on my crosstown walks to and from work. In the afternoons, in city heat as hard as cement, I passed lines of people wrapped around a dozen midtown blocks, waiting to pay their respects, holding white paper water cups from the Salvation Army and leaving them empty as votive offerings marking every step along the pilgrimage.

***

The year was not even half over. If not already or by the coming summer, then certainly by its last day, 1968 would join 1939, 1929, 1848, 1815, and all the other quanta that spiked the continuum. I thought it was a gift. The Chinese wish it as a curse: "May you live in interesting times."

***

31

The bombs bursting in error

Even the home front was in harm's way then. Across the street from a friend's apartment on West 11th Street, just around the corner from Richard M. Nixon's Fifth Avenue *pied-à-terre*, a bomb factory townhouse blew up. "Oooops...BOOM": bombers and building pulverized to a mound of granules. I buffed the FDNY overhaul the next day.

At work, several times we were told to leave our desks and wait outside on the sidewalk until the cops could check out the latest bomb threat — routine pro-Biafran protest lodged against the Ugandan consulate in the building. Once, my group head and I decided that again it was just a hoax, so let's stay and finish up some radio spots. Then a cop stuck his head in: "Hey, you. You're *leaving*. NOW," punctuated by a nightstick rim shot on the door frame.

Even closer to home....

 The Night They Banged Alma Mater

[Acronym, quite coincidentally, "TNTBAM."]

Dead center on the Columbia campus is a bronze neo-classi*kitsch* statue of a 10-foot *zaftig* woman seated with arms extended, laurel wreath on her head, thin torch in her right hand, and somewhere hidden in the folds of her robe, if you can find it, and I for one cannot, an owl. On her pedestal, "ALMA MATER."[*] Sometime early in the '60s, the administration in the imposing Roman bathetic library behind her planned to gild the statue. She stayed greenish. In 1968, after the uprising and police putdown, she wore splats of red and black paint and around her neck a placard:

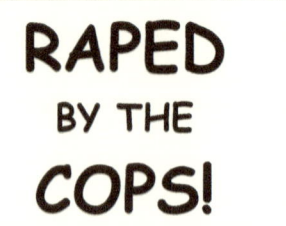

RAPED
BY THE
COPS!

---

[*] From the song of the same name, to the tune of (no kidding) *"Deutschland Über Alles,"*

Mother stayed on rock eternal/Crowned and set upon a height....

That was metaphor. I witnessed a felonious assault.

On May 14, 1970, at 4:17 on a cloudless Manhattan morning, someone tried to kill my Alma Mama. They slipped a fat gob of plastique under her dress, and later the explosive went off with the CRACKboomboom of a dud for-real firework fired at altitude zero feet. The sound woke people twenty blocks south and brought half a thousand students out in their pajamas to stand before her and wonder.

The blast blew a foot-wide wound in the small of her back, and moved all three tons of her bronze benevolence five inches closer to Harlem. Some people say she rocked back and forth like a Joe Palooka punching bag. And her dress will never be the same. Alma is a plump brazen woman but they kicked the living daylights out of her with just one shot. I know. That shot almost kicked the living daylights out of me. My date and I were twenty feet away, the only people on the plaza, when the bomb cut loose. A few days later a sergeant from the 2-6th Precinct told my girlfriend, in a friendly and reassuring way, "If youse'da been on the other side when that baby popped, I wouldn't wanna be around to scrape youse up."

Let me explain a little about my date. Annapurna was the daughter of the Prime Minister's personal physician. She had been dandled on the knee of Jawaharlal Nehru. Annapurna, Barnard '70, was a Dravidian Brahmin named after a mountain, named after a goddess, and she acted that way. Once she handed me her coat and said "Please hold this. Think of it as the white man's burden." Of course, after a shower together, I told her I had secretly baptized her a Catholic.

Annapurna that night wore a sari that was six yards' worth of shocking pink silk edged in black and metallic gold. We had attended the traditionally extravagant college yearbook dinner, followed by a special-invitation-only post-prandial taste-testing of recreational controlled substances. She hardly indulged, but we both wanted to keep walking around to enjoy our giddiness and spring-fevered delirium.

In Morningside Park Annapurna stood like the Black Madonna against that ghastly red-orange glow that rises sourceless in clumps from cities at night and hangs, brooding and beating, loitering in the way of the stars, until all of a sudden the red-orange blanches and up comes the false dawn. But I think I was looking more at Harlem than at her, because at four in the morning, with its soft sodium yellow streets and stoplights stopping nobody, Harlem can be a very pretty place. And Columbia, as we moved hand-in-hand very slowly back across campus to take Annapurna home, Columbia was beautiful.

We stood close together one flight of stairs below Alma Mater. Here I was with the two most extraordinary women I had ever known, and I was stoned enough to wish eternity on myself.

The whole sky turned pure white — then orange for seconds and seconds and seconds. "Nuke" was the best word my head could get out. I slipped my arm around Annapurna just as the shock rattled my lungs like paper bags, slapped us back, shook loose everything we had as we clutched and trembled, trembled for minutes and could not stop the shaking.

"Oh my God, I am heartily sorry for having offended Thee, and I detest all my sins because I dread the loss of Heaven and the pains of Hell...." I had not said an Act of Contrition — it is the best prayer to have in your throat when you buy the farm — since my Catholicism had lapsed at puberty, but I was not doing a bad job now recalling and meaning every word, because Old Mister Death was bearing down on us like a subway train from a station away late at night out in the boonies. "Annapurna," I said, "the University is blowing up."

I was stoned but I got straight in seconds flat. We turned and watched a thick column of smoke, a fat white interruption in the darkness, rise over Alma Mater, lope along the plaza and just above the crests of a hundred yards of new tulips. Around the corner a walkie-talkie yapped and a big campus cop came charging down the stairs right at us. He was hollering "All units come to Alma Mater" over and over into the radio, and from what war movies tell me about scared, he was *scared*.

The campus cops came, followed by the real cops in six radio cars, with a full-box response of fire trucks pulling up along Broadway. Then there were on the plaza some five hundred young men in pajamas like some giant outdoor slumber party. Annapurna and I stood there, the only fully-dressed civilians in the crowd, just watching and still shaking, until one of the pinstriped pajamas said

"Gee, Wiz, I expected you to get bombed at the dinner, but this is ridiculous."

Then the first cop who ever laid a hand on me in my life moved my elbow courteously but with a lot of emphasis and halfway up the stairs got around to asking, "Would you like to come with me and answer some questions?"

In the Security Office we waited and watched the night officer, a lawyer who worked the shift for the sake of the action and his incurable insomnia, with two phones stuck in his ears, a pencil clamped in his teeth and a mug whiter than the ceramic tile walls. "Look, I don't care if your lock's busted. I can't help you. Sleep in the lobby tonight. We've just been bombed here." "No, I'm not Kathy Kelly in Plimpton. We've just been bombed here." "I know a loud noise woke you up. We've just been bombed here. Go back to sleep."

Eventually we got to give our stories. Our cop confided that he really didn't think we did it. You betcha, officer. Your average mad bomber does not wear an royal blue Oleg Cassini shirt, buck-fifty red polka dot Tie City tie, red-striped double-breasted navy blazer, and Nunn Bush monk strap wingtip loafers with thick gold buckles. Maybe your average racetrack tout. Not even in disguise would a Weatherman want to be caught dead duked out like that. Especially not with a slimline black matte vinyl attaché case.

On our way out we saw a guard yelling at the kids moving in for a closer look. "YOU ALL WANNA GET KILLED?" he asked, knowing that there could be unexploded charges simmering in the rubble and a Texas tower hunter sighting in his Mauser out there in the night. Annapurna took one look at the shards of bronze and stone and the burns and jagged holes in that great lady and took me in tow doubletime.

We sat in the garden as the sky lit up and I told her we were maybe the luckiest two people in all New York that day. We were a little put out that nobody made us heroes but we each figured privately that had we been on Alma's other side, or even right in front of her, we woulda had two dead kids on our hands. I still half-consider every day the Big Fella has given me since then a free and clear gift. And thank you, Sir, for letting me stick around for the Big Show.

35

(Flash forward a decade — alcohol detox unit, St. Francis General Hospital, Pittsburgh; Rabbi Abraham J. Twerski, M.D., Chief of Psychiatry and stunt double for the Old Testament Deity: "For some reason, whatever it is, God must want Jimmy Wisniewski around a little longer." A reminder well worth repeating, Abe. Every day above ground is a good one.)

***

 First sedition

At the Armed Forces Examination, Classification, and Induction Center at 39 Whitehall Street, down at the tip of Manhattan within view of the harbor, I took — and failed — my Vietnam-era draft physical. Actually, I was classified I-Y — not absolutely rejected as entirely unfit, but available in case of a (last ditch, no-tomorrow, now-or-never, sudden-death-overtime, bottom-of-the-barrel, *Volksturm*) national emergency. The exam and the events gave me a timely story; I already had a title, taken from the first thing that greeted the daily straggle of apprehensive 18-year-old men entering 39 Whitehall Street — one outsized, neck-stiffening, reality-slap metal sign:

> # THE SECURITY OF WORLD PEACE BEGINS HERE

For the story, I had to have an illustration of that, plus a few architectural details, along with some human interest impressions of the resident armed forces and transient short-armed conscripts. For an illustrator, I had Gail Tarre (pronounced as in "rip," but sometimes self-styled as in *lacrimae*), California *Gaia* gal with a most appropriate, softly stark monochrome graphic style.

The last piece we worked on was a series of campus-area restaurant reviews which rated the establishments not with stars or spoons but cockroaches. (The only place that merited "NO COCKROACHES" turned out to be Tom's on Broadway, since then the establishment-shot exterior of the coffee shop in "Seinfeld.") Gail needed a model cockroach, which I volunteered to capture — no easy

36

pickings to get one big enough for her to visualize in detail, unsquashed, unscathed, naturalistically intact. But no lack of quarry, either.

Gail put on her muumuu, hung her beads, wove her braids, packed up her pad, and went downtown to sketch some 39 Whitehall images. The soldiers were very nice, she said. Of course they were. Both she and the vista down her neckline were remarkably nice. So there she was, cheerfully charcoaling away, when who should tap her on the shoulder but an NYPD sergeant from the 1st Precinct, who asked what she was doing there. Then she was invited to come over to the station house for a chat.

Unbeknownst to either of us, 39 Whitehall Street had been bombed or Molotoved quite recently — evidently not much damage but obviously much more vigilance. Thus, since Gail

(1) looked, dressed, acted, and talked like the counterculture incarnate, and

(2) was altogether too upbeat and pleasant for a stereotypically intense New York artist, and consequently was likely

    a) drugged, and/or

    b) brainwashed, and/or

    c) foreign, and/or

    d) acting, and

(3) was drawing pictures inside a U.S. military installation during a time of national disorder, now therefore, she was subversive and suspect.

The interrogation, she related, went on for about an hour, mostly small talk with the sergeant and a duet of detectives. Then they got to the point.

"You can't be researching illustrations for a college yearbook. College yearbooks don't use stuff like that. What are you doing really?"

"Researching illustrations for a college yearbook."

"OK, honey, who's your boss? Who are you working for?"

"I'm not sure what his real name is, but everyone calls him 'Wizard.'"

"'Wizard'?"

"'Wizard.' Or 'Wiz.'"

"Is he black? Is he some kinda black militant or one of those radicals up there?"

"I think he's Polish. And he works for an ad agency."

***

Culture *shlock*ed

The moment I got the job I instantly became a *de facto* adult and a dues-paying, card-carrying, member-in-good-standing of the real world. But I was still a minor and a dope-smoking, bleeding-heart liberal artisan, a plainclothes infiltrator from too far up the Upper West Side literally to count. (Colleagues from the 'burbs or the East Side never thought much higher than 72nd Street, or much past Central Park West.)

Every day I got to live at least 1½ lives in two utterly disparate worlds. From *ad hoc* caucuses to ad biz, the switches took some getting used to:

WEST SIDE	EAST SIDE
Cut 9:00 class; all-nighters	9 to 5
Tie-dyes [1]	Ties
Munchies	Expense account lunches
Hair	Tickets to *Hair*
Rhetoric	Verbage[2]
Mantras, chants	Jingles
Manifestos	Memos
Demonstrations	Product demos
Collegiality, participatory democracy[3]	Dog-and-pony shows, brainstorming
Seminars, colloquia, bull sessions, rallies	Meetings, meetings, still more meetings
The Media	Media buys
Civilization	Demographics
Issues	Copy points
Causes	Accounts
Offensives	Campaigns
Weltanschauung	Creative strategy
Transcripts	Paychecks

---

1 Typically crafted by girlfriend in bathtub; sometimes used in lieu of Rorschach test
2 Client term for copy, variation on "verbiage"
3 Everybody all talks at once.

Adspeak *se habla aquí*

People in advertising talked almost as much as people in academia, and the language was just as distinct a dialect. "Not quite right" meant "Wrong." "A few little nitpicks" meant "Let's rewrite it." "I like it" meant "I don't like it." "Great!" was "OK," "Good" was "Not too good," and "Interesting" was "I don't understand it, so the Client sure won't, and whether I understand it or not, I don't like it."

Both the ideas and their expression comprised an advanced education in themselves. Just a few verbatims from meetings, memos, work requests, hallway huddles and cocktail colloquia:

"For this, we envision a gal who is wacky and zany but mod."

"Let's make sure we're all gnawing on the same bone."

"It's a mute point."

"A good execution cannot save a bad idea, but a bad execution can kill a good idea."

"We can't cast a female bloodhound. Their teats sag worse than my granny's."

"That tie skews young."

"You used the same word twice. I thought you're not supposed to do that."

"The copy doesn't haven't enough sparkle."

"Right in the middle of the meeting, [Client] broke down and started crying and said 'The Agency doesn't love me any more. You don't care about me or my products. *I* care about my products.'"

"Animation? I wouldn't go that far."

"If you can't say anything, say 'It's great.' Even better, 'It's special.' Or 'It's *really* special.'"

"Frank Zappa? Who is Frank Zappa?"

"[Client] said 'I want somebody fired for this!' So I sent him a résumé of this media gal who just left. I hope he feels guilty."

"Great concept, but it's ahead of their time."

"She's too...black."

"We're running out of runway."

"[Assoc. Creative Director] hasn't had an idea in 10 years."

"Actually, he keeps having the same idea."

"So [Client] said 'You're a liar,' hung up. Half hour later, he called again, said 'I'm sorry. You're not a liar. [Your associate] is a liar."

"Change 'Pass the bucks' to 'Pass the dollars.'"

"You're having a serious attack of the cutesies."

"The stuff tastes like hell, but that's never been an obstacle for us before, has it?"

"Let's do something 'Bonnie and Clyde' [or other most-recently-seen movie]."

"If this is the way we wanted it writ, we would have writ it ourselves."

"[The Client] won't approve any woman we cast unless she looks like his wife."

"It's too...blue."

"We gotta get in bed with these guys."

"Let's put it in the bar car and see if it floats off at Darien."

"Not a sentence!!!!!"

"Not a sentence either!!!!!"

"The Client *loved* everything. Of course, the Client didn't *buy* anything."

"The lawyers will let us say '*OUR PRODUCT, TOO, IS NOT WITHOUT MERIT.*'"

"It's too...addy."

"Any more legal changes and we'll be left with '*COMPLIMENTS OF A FRIEND.*'"

"Every day I get down on my knees and thank God He did not make me an account executive [or TV producer or Client or media rep.]"

"This is advertising. We can do whatever we want."

And many, many more.

***

The Name on the Door

"Mr. Bayles would like to see you in his office as soon as possible."

"Yes ma'am. Just lemme put on a tie and I'll be right down. Uh, where is his office, exactly?"

"Oh, 12th floor, right off the elevator. Can't miss it. You really don't have to wear a tie."

"I better anyway. After all, this is my first chance to meet the man. Won't take but a minute."

The real trouble was that my (burnt orange, Brooks Bros., hand-me-down-from-a-friend) shirt was missing a button halfway down the front; the tie more or less concealed that. So, wearing a loosely knotted brown burlappy tie, noticeably undone but negligibly open shirt collar, I tore down the stairs, where an upward bound account guy gave me a wide berth on a landing. "I always move over for a fast man."

"Heagan Bayles just called."

"Well, we don't want to keep him waiting now, do we?"

S. Heagan Bayles was the agency's last name, chairman and co-founder, the "B" (first initial I ever met in the business) in SSCand (no ampersand) B Inc., originally Sullivan, Stauffer, Colwell & Bayles, established 1946, two years before I was born, and now the world's sixth-largest advertising agency. He was calling in response to the following from the Vice President, Personnel:

MEMO

FROM   Bill Timm   **DATE**   December 22, 1970

We are planning a surprise Bulletin Board saluting Doc Brennan at the time of his retirement mid-January.

Along with his photograph we will include short quoted statements of reminiscence or praise from those who have been associated with him.

We would appreciate your jotting down a sentence or two on this sheet and returning it to me. Thank you.

One of my nicer ideas. Old Mark volunteered me to write the bulletin boards, monthly intramural displays hung in wood and glass cases on each floor, since he had been dragooned to do the graphics. In December, he thought of collections of children's art, which is exhibited in every workplace and all looks alike. I added the head,

From our house to your house —
From all of us to all of you —
The happiest of holidays

The tag was a natural:

God bless us, every one!

The next idea got bigger than I bargained for. Thomas F. ("Doc") Brennan, 70, starched white hair, plush pink face, beanbag waistline, had become beloved in fifty years in advertising — extraordinary longevity and venerability in a business where age fifty was a milestone (or headstone) and "He's a nice guy" was estimable praise. Legend had it that when Doc was copy chief at the great radio agency, Ruthrauff & Ryan, he gave Bayles his first job.

On this job, from all I knew after working with him a few months, Doc wrote the occasional odds-and-ends accessory assignment for S&H Green Stamps — radio tags, supermarket bagstuffers, cover letters and such. Every morning, four or five of us would sit in his office to trade overnight stories and the joke-of-the-day over our cardboard Chock Full o' Nuts cups. On summer afternoons, his standing alibi for AWOL was feeding the monkeys in the Central Park Zoo. As he was cleaning out his office, he presented me with his thesaurus, contents spilling out of a back-broken threadbare binding: "Not that you'd need it, but a writer's supposed to have one." Classy fella — another exceptional epithet in the business.

Down to the newly neocolonialized 12th floor (the decor prompted Bill Weithas to ask "Where's the body?"). I shuffle ceremoniously into the outer office of the Chairman and Founder, to be admitted immediately through a large anteroom. Here, several young, attractive people whom I have never seen before are confabbing at a conference table and blatantly broadcasting eavesdroppable buzzwords: "Marshall McLuhan ...U-235...IBM System 360...*pro bono* Urban Coalition."

S. Heagan Bayles, tall, bald, solemn, comes out to shake my hand. Then he says sharply to the conferees, "Get that pack of Marlboros off the table! We have cigarette business, but not that kind!"

[Back then, even as cigarette commercials were about to be banned from the American air, smoking was not only permitted but approved and indeed tacitly encouraged in our workplace. After all, the American Tobacco Company — Pall Mall® Gold, Green, and Red, plus Lucky Strike® Filters, Maryland™ and assorted new product intros — was the biggest account in the shop. This amounted to fully one-quarter of the Agency's income, a responsibility which required everyone from the president to the pasteup intern to respond "How high?" and "When may I come down?" when that Client said "Jump."

[As a direct consequence: employees who smoked cigarettes were expected to keep a pack of the Client's product on their desks or on their persons. Those products which the Agency handled were preferred, and in fact available at near wholesale prices via weekly orders through the receptionists, but any American brand would do — Carlton®, for ultra-low-tar... dual-filter Tareyton®, for people who would rather fight than switch (violent brand loyalty dramatized by BBDO in ads depicting smokers with black eyes) ... Lucky Strike® ("IT'S TOASTED," "So round, so firm, so fully packed," the cryptic "L.S./M.F.T. — Lucky Strike Means Fine Tobacco"), for WWII nostalgia, downscale *macho*, yellow fingers and a systemic sensation of the respiratory tract with every puff. Only the package and brand I.D. mattered: if you really liked Chesterfield® ("Not a cough in a carload"), you could stuff them into your Pall Mall pack, or Camel® into your deck of Luckies. Also permissible, American Cigars — popular-priced Antonio y Cleopatra or luxury aluminum-tubed La Corona. On my desk, between my fingers, in my mouth, habitually and heavily, I always had the original unfiltered Pall Mall Red ("America's leading *straight* cigarette.")

[Given my own dependence, I was especially impressed with the insider info that the Client's senior managers had all given up

45

smoking, but lit and held — just *held*, didn't smoke! — cigarettes at such public occasions as shareholder meetings. Then again, this Client was lineally descended from the legendary George Washington Hill, who inspired the Sidney Greenstreet character in *The Hucksters*. Hill's rules for advertising still stood as our creative rubrics and art directors' ordeals: "Always show a big pack. Show a big open pack pointed at the reader. Always set the brand name and headline in the typeface used on the package. Repeat the sales message frequently. Repeat the brand name frequently." Per Carl Sandburg:

"Irritate 'em, irritate 'em,"said the ghost of George Washington Hill.

[Writing for tobacco was entrusted to a few elite specialists. One great line could make a reputation. For instance, Bernie Sloan, my group head, wrote "Come to where the flavor is" for Marlboro when he was with Leo Burnett in Chicago. He didn't create the cowboy or even "Come to Marlboro Country" — just the lead, "Come to where the flavor is." Bernie made his bones with that. Gene Whelan was renowned for Pall Mall Gold's "Longer, yet milder," a *non sequitur* if I ever heard one. I'm not sure who all took the credit for the sex- and statement-laden, upbeat and bouncy jingle,

You make out better at both ends

With The Big Tip — Pall Mall Gold!

but the cigarette broadcast ban kicked in before it became hummable mass Muzak, or lit up or snuffed out careers.

[People working on cigarette accounts were greatly valued, richly rewarded, and thoroughly scared — the shakiest people in a spasmodically insecure business. They stood or staggered by maybe six fundamental principles:

a) 1 (or 1.5 or 2.0) out of 10 smokers was switchable (roughly the same fraction as beer and booze);

b) Reaching those smokers and thus increasing market share required the expenditure of countless millions of Client dollars;

c) Client's stated purpose: to create a product with a salable difference;

d) Agency's assigned mission: to create the sales messages to convey that unique distinction — but

e) Client declined to divulge sales figures to Agency, so nobody ever really knew where they stood;

f) Agency's status, stability, and hundreds of jobs depended on the tobacco business.

Small wonder that the account showed high rates of casualties, morbidity, indeed, mortality. A few people unexpectedly "resigned to pursue other interests," we would be informed by memos on everyone's desks first thing in the morning. Account executives and traffic managers typically were obsessive, compulsive, and hypomanic. When one management supervisor suddenly died, and the next became incapacitated, I met the next one and literally hoped he would survive. Even the pasteup guy suffered constant gastric distress and periodic disease.

[Public health never arose as an issue, nor did ethics ever present an obstacle. Anyone who had social or moral qualms knew to keep them quiet. Supposedly, people in other unnamed shops who had declined to work on cigarette assignments were promptly shown the elevator down.

[I did have to do a little ciggie stuff — briefly, reluctantly, dutifully, curiously. A new and interesting experience, in fact. The product: new Maryland, with the Made-For-Menthol™ Blend, tobacco that was slowly and naturally air-cured, not flue-cured like the stuff in ordinary cigarettes. On the pack, a pastoral fox-hunting illustration (presumably a Maryland scene), which also dominated the ads, with formulaic headlines and three or four sentences of body copy covering three or four essential copy points. Not much of a creative challenge, but the demands were revolving, ongoing, drop-everything, crash-priority, immediate turnaround, otherwise unheard-of deadlines. If they asked for it in the morning, they expected it in the afternoon.

[Client feedback on intro sales: "It's a slow starter." Uh-oh.

[For creative exercise, I did get an exploratory (i.e., busywork, wheelspinning, flying blind, shot-in-the-dark, hit-or-miss, uncannily prophetic) assignment: "What if we can't say *anything* about the product?" Solutions: classic quotations about "gold," "green," "red," "lucky," etc.; blind heads like "Enough said," "No other cigarette can make this statement," "What else can we say?", "Beyond words," and "---- ---- ---- ----!"]

***

Heagan Bayles' bare desk is a 10-foot elliptical expanse, one sheet of black marble inset with two lead crystal ashtrays. Against the far wall is a red and gold Chinese Chippendale breakfront the size of a small house. After Heagan ascertains the sense of the business at hand, he calls in a secretary and dictates a flawless, fluent *ex tempore* commentary, historical and personal. In a few spots his voice catches and quavers. Respectfully, I look away. I also take notes, since many mentions are legendary (Hopkins, Schwab) or obscure ("Jimmy Tennyson, worthy of his namesake....")

The secretary leaves to transcribe the shorthand and we get to small-talk-while-u-wait. I light a Pall Mall and ask polite toadyish background questions. Mostly Heagan reminisces, lobbing up allusions demonstrating that he knows where I come from, where and what I studied, what I've done for his shop lately, even what I like, right on down to Hemingway and the top brand of beer in Pittsburgh.

<<Wha? Where's the Tele-Promp-Ter®?>>

The secretary returns with a typescript, takes his verbal edits, and the chitchat resumes. By this time I am slouched in the chair, leg draped over an arm, taking a note and a puff now and then, beginning to feel both easy and outright important, not to mention real impressed. ("I was talking with the Chairman of the Board the other day....") He checks the revised typescript and says he hopes it will serve my purposes. I thank him for his thoughts, and for such definitive, exclusive detail.

"Sir, there's one more thing for which I guess we will need your permission. On the bulletin board, we should like to temporarily rename the Agency 'Sullivan, Stauffer, Colwell & Brennan.'" He chuckled. "Of course."

I went back upstairs walleyed and slackjawed "I just spent a half hour with Heagan Bayles," I murmured to Jack Thwaites, the oldest hand around. "How does he do it? How did he know ...?"

"Heagan never talks to strangers."

***

The tribute filled up with twenty-five people's testimonials about Doc. Dick Uhl, the Creative Director, who got his start writing Princeton varsity shows and kept his Clio awards atop an upright piano, flanking the placard

SELLING SPOKEN HERE

sent a note opening with

Dear Doc:

> *You were Top Copy man at Ruthrauff and Ryan when I checked into their checking department as a trainee in 1939. Thirty-one years later as you check out of SSC&B you're still the Top....*

and then sent his secretary to make sure I *stet*ted the upper case "T"s. I sent her back with sheet music to the Clancy Brothers and Tommy Makem's "Brennan On The Moor," suggesting that Dick might consider a performance at Doc's farewell racket, meantime expecting or hoping that Dick would also think to sanitize the lyric so as not to give offense to Doc's West Indian junior copywriter apprentice.

Bill Timm rolled his eyes as he handed me one note. "This is from the Old Man":

I could say a lot of nice things about Doc Brennan but I shall confine myself to one -- which I can say with great sincerity and which will be most meaningful to him.

Doc is a real pro in the finest tradition of our business.

-- Alfred J. Seaman, President

<<This could be tightened up a little bit. Nah. Better not.>>

I did get in the last words:

You taught me to start trusting people over thirty.

You taught me that I have a half century of growing up to do before I could ever hope to fill brogans as big as yours.

And you are teaching me right now that writing isn't quite as easy as it looks. All our best men and women put their best words on this bulletin board. All these words from all these people still cannot say what we want to say. Words fail.

- Jim Wisniewski

***

49

James Casimir Wisniewski

[*Memnoir*]

Henceforth this will start seeming Kafkaesque (I guess, not having read much Kafka.) It will sound like fiction, fantasy, fable. Advertising notwithstanding, I do not know how to write that sort of stuff. I suspect that if it were fiction, it would hang together a lot better and go down a lot easier.

Take it as fiction or any way you want. However you take it does not change whatever it was. In any case, every name is actual, every quote is verbatim or very close, every fact is checkable. As Prof. Stengel put it, you could look it up.

Nonetheless, what happened here is not how business is done, not even in advertising. This gets bigger than it has any right to be, and so events begin assuming mythic if not epic proportions. And no, it may not make sense — not to me, much less to you. And yes, I heard voices, but not from inside my head. And I concede that some if not most of the story will appear to be hallucinatory. But if apparitions, they were solids. If delusions, they are detailed. If madness, it is seamless, impervious, adamantly permanent.

Then: did I imagine entire momentous months? Now: how does this illusion last — at length, in depth, in full, phono- and photographically in memory, absolutely ineradicably — for more than half my life?

***

Mr. ZIP®

Without warning or apparent cause, on or about January 12, 1971, I suddenly found myself somewhere between *persona non grata* and unperson. People were walking past my office door and floating disconcerting remarks:

"Just plain immaturity, that's all."

"Like we really need a radical in this place."

"Maybe they can talk that way up there, but not down here."

"Nobody wants a troublemaker around."

"You wonder what he's on."

"Smartass. Wiseguy. Comedian."

"What's he doing here anyway?"

"Remember what happened to that fella, whatsisname, Mike Turner. He tried to…."

Old Mark snubs me. Hardly anybody even looks at me. I am being shunned. Leslee Smoke calls and says she's having her period so I shouldn't call her. Donna Nicholas, Leslee's roommate, modern dancer and feisty fantasy, calls and says she's going to be working on a paper, so she's busy, not that I asked. Judy Appleton, my closest kindred spirit from college, who's been out of touch for a year, calls and says she now has a job in the city. "Jimmy, I can see your office from mine," but won't say where she is. Interoffice mail includes a packet of sugar sent by "Shirley Fine."

<<Jeez. All of a sudden. Everybody. Somebody wanna tell me what I did? Hey, I'm sorry.>>

"You guys going to lunch?"

"Er, yeah."

"Ya wouldn't mind some company?"

"Jim, it's, kinda, invitation only."

"Oh. OK. You're being took. Where ya goin'?"

"The Cloud Club."

"Oh."

[The Cloud Club in the Krupp-steel pinnacle of the Chrysler Building, via polished paneled private elevator express from the lobby. Just happened upon it myself one Saturday afternoon: snuck in with the yearbook photo editor, Jon Kandel, packing a Russian Widelux™ 35mm x 3-frame panoramic camera to shoot skyline photos. I held Jon by his belt — fortunately he was smallish and skinny — as he hung out the windows. ("Wiz, if you lose your grip or I start to go, grab for the Widelux first. I'm insured, it isn't.") We had never before seen, been surrounded by, so much city, smack in the center, 42nd and Fifth. For souvenirs I swiped matchbooks and a monogrammed Club spoon, which I placed in my medicine chest, both for Pepto-Bismol® and the Beatles' line "She came in through the bathroom window, protected by a silver spoon...."]

During lunch, through the metal walls of the conference room came "Teach Your Children Well," Crosby Stills & Nash, several times over. From what I could see, the conference room was all dark. Then more hallway overhearings:

"600 pages of letters...."

"So we say 'We have this kid writer here who is a really, really heavy user of your service.'"

"We already have stamp business."

"This guy is now our new business department."

"What if he does that with *their* stationery?"

"They'll have to give it to him."

<<Huh? What the fuck is going on here?>>

Then Don Booth, Creative Senior VP and the man who wrote "Wonder® Bread builds strong bodies 8 ways" (four more ways since discovered) glided into my office. "Did you get a receipt from our lunch with Doc?" (At Charles *à la Pomme Soufflé*. Doc ordered his martini with a cherry, which is what "Wisniewski" means in Polish. Booth, uncharacteristically, had to leave lunch early, so I picked up the tab, cash.)

"I ate it."

"Don't be silly. The Agency pays for it."

"I ate it."

"How much was it?"

"$50 with tip."

He shook his head, handed me the money, and left. My old pal and patron Don Booth, who regularly would take us to lunch and get us loaded...who once had me try on his suitcoat...who once was short of cash so the 1st National Bank of Wisniewski lent him two double sawbucks on the spot...who once in fun tried to pick my pocket, easy enough to deflect with the New York swim-twist maneuver ("Just wanted to see where you kept your wallet") ...Don Booth, who said the way to get something done is "Just drop it in somebody's lap" ...who often had me summon people on his behalf because my voice is profoundly imperative ("You big phony," he joked) ...who made me practically a fixture on his couch by the door ...who had described a former top colleague at Ted Bates as the big boss's doorstop. I was Don Booth's doorstop.

Then Cy Nathan, Senior VP and Creative Services Administrator, stopped by, smiled, chuckled, and said "Hal Rover wants your stopwatch." Hal Rover was third or fourth in command. First I was tickled: I did like to jog up and down stairs and through corridors. But — my stopwatch, the broadcast writer's standard left-hand indispensable equipment, brand name "Minerva," back engraved with the Agency initials and "#27." That — that's almost like asking for my badge and gun.

Then the usual group is sitting in Doc's office underneath my freshly produced Doc Brennan tribute bulletin board poster. He had just ducked out for the afternoon. Carmen LaFont, Doc's plus-size secretary, stops in wearing his tweed hat and raglan raincoat. "Hey, are you in drag, Carmencita?", someone asks. "I'm taking them down to him in the parking garage. He called from down there and said he forgot them." Then Del the Receptionist comes in and reads the poster, wiggling her ass emphatically, excessively, obviously, corkscrewing right in front of my nose. I look at Vinnie; he lifts his monk-strap-shod foot and lowers it emphatically. "Buckle down, Winsocki."

<<Moral support. Now I know something's going on, but I can't ask what. Keep on going as if nothing's happened. Not hard. I don't flinch at much.>>

At the end of the afternoon, big bald Lou Menna, old pro art boss, is in Cy's office and I can hear them from down the hall. "...experience in Chrysler Aircraft, U.S. Treasury, Hughes Tool...." "...send a boy to do a man's job...." "...a very talented writer...." "...don't care for some of his language." I soon understand that the exchange is for my ears and my benefit, since they are talking *à la* Sid Stone — intelligible phrases amid passable garble. Soon I begin to get what it's about.

Last piece I saw on Lou's drawing board was a speculative ad, full page broadsheet newspaper, headlined

TODAY THE UNITED STATES POST OFFICE BECOMES THE U.S. POSTAL SERVICE,

with a currency engraver's ultrafine rendering of the General Post Office on 8th Avenue; as the subhead, all across the building, the cliché postal motto carved in stone. So we were pitching the Postal Service account — $17 mill worth of business — and I had something to do with our capabilities.

Aha. OK. Got it. Letters. I write a lot of letters. Somebody earlier said 600 pages. Yeah. Come to think of it, sounds about right. Total might add up to that or more. Of course. Makes perfect sense. "Not only do we have stamp business [S&H Green Stamps] — why, we have this young writer who is an exceptional postal patron. In fact, here are more than 600 pages of his letters that we've collected."

Now I get it. So this must be a test. A setup. A demo. A stunt. A surprise. Something like that. Looking north, I can see a bright light in a window of that black glazed tower. Judy, huh? Ready as I'll ever be.

In the lobby there is a metal multicompartmented locker. As I head out the front, the security guard opens the freight entrance door at the side. Right outside on Lexington Avenue there is an office moving van. The subway comes right away.

Uptown bound on the 7th Avenue IRT, some swishy guy, or a girl in business drag, makes an obvious and inept attempt to pick my pocket. I twist away and brace my butt against the car door. He gets off at the next stop. Then a woman makes a pass at the pants, but again, an amateur dip, and she looks like an account service secretary, Donna Somebody-Or-Other in an undeceiving disguise.

Before I realize it, the train is standing on the platform above 125th and Broadway, doors staying open until it crosses my mind that, oh, yeah, I get off here.

That's the cue. This is it. Here we go. I can take a hint. Mike the Mailman said it. I head straight for the mailbox at the foot of Tiemann Place and drop in my wallet and keys.

Now what?

First, half a block up, I get into my apartment building easily enough, with people coming or going and opening the front security door. In front of my apartment, I find empty cans of Schaefer beer and New Iberia Vienna sausages. I think I hear someone inside the place, so I knock and rattle the door loud enough that a fella across the way sticks his head out. I duck around the corner. Probably a good idea to go for a walk and figure out what I'm supposed to do.

Hostile hard January night. Up the street to Grant's Tomb — "LET US HAVE PEACE" atop the columnar entry. This is one of the safest places anywhere in the city parkland, a federal reservation under 24-hour guard, so I take a walk all the way around. OK. Gimme a hint. Whaddaya want? Where's the party? Then I see two guys half a block away, where two guys usually shouldn't be.

"Hey, brothers. Lookin' for a place to stay."

"There's a black hotel on 125th Street, brother."

"There's a Puerto Rican hotel on 110th Street, man."

"Thanks, but I guess not. Maybe I'll go sleep with General and Mrs. Grant."

Just keep moving — along Riverside Drive, down LaSalle, on Claremont, back and forth and over again in the cold until I return to Broadway and the 125th Street IRT station, go up the escalator, across, down the escalator, around and around this 4-story Ferris wheel, pausing in the station lobby to warm up a little. The Transit Authority cop on post conspicuously turns his back.

Again up my block, I see people going into my building. "At least it's a warm place," one says. Another one is carrying a long package containing a police-type lock with the brand name "JIMMY." But this time I can't get in the front door, so I head to 125th Street and on a hunch, around the corner to Old Broadway.

Aha. The Post Office, Manhattanville Station, New York, NY 10027. I start to mosey around the mail trucks at the loading dock, but in like 15 seconds an alarm bell starts ringing, red lights are flashing, and two guys brandishing badges come running out yelping. Guess not. If not here, then....

2-6 Precinct, NYPD, just a few doors down. Why not? Not many alternatives left. This place is all white gloss tile, intense shadowless light and a cop out front at a steel desk.

"Whaddaya here for?"

"Officer, I lost my wallet and my keys and I just need someplace to stay."

He hollers toward the back, "Call the wagon."

"Naw, officer, I didn't mean it that way."

"So what *did* you mean?"   Whereupon I tell him about the pickpocket attempts on the subway and how somebody told me that I should dump my valuables into a mailbox if that ever happens. He shakes his head and makes faces throughout the story.

"You have a job?"

"Yeah. Ad agency, Midtown."

"Did your bosses have a fight today?"

<<WHA?>>

"Er, uh, yeah. But people are always fighting about something down there." "Did they have a fight about *you*?"

<<WHA?>>

"Mighta been. I dunno. Yeah. Coulda. Sounded like it."

"What's your address again?"

"4-5 Tiemann Place, 6-F."

"Write down your phone number for me."

I write "**666-9796**" and he reads "'**666-N...N**.' That's not a phone number. I can't read that."   My handwriting has been marginally legible since grade school, but it can't be that bad.

"Where'd you live before you moved up here?"

"110$^{\underline{th}}$ and Broadway, SRO. Single room occupancy."

"You're just a roomer. A *rumor*. Nobody knows you around here."

<<GULP>>

"If ya need a place to stay, I'll call the wagon for ya. Otherwise you can get outta here and stop wasting the New York City Police Department's time."

"OK, officer. But, uh, don't I get to make one phone call?"

He points to a pay phone on the wall.

"Uh, I don't have a dime."

He points to the *Daily News* jammed in my overcoat pocket. "You got a dime."

OK, now what? This isn't working out. As I am leaving, shaking my head and staring at my Corfam® shoetops, cop in a winter tunic and moustache stops me. "What happened?" He sounds like he wants to know.

"Aw, officer, jeez, I dunno," and replay the whole story in one long sentence.

"Here's a thought. Why don't ya just go home?"

"Sure. Think I need a police escort?"

"Just go across the street by the buses there. Go to the emergency there."

"Hey, thanks, officer." I want to shake his hand but he starts putting on green gimmicked gloves, and another much bigger cop is tapping the stairway handrail with his nightstick.

Across the street by the buses is a police department callbox. On top is an empty bottle. The emergency. Cute. Very funny. Or maybe that's a good sign. Maybe that means the party is well under way.

It is getting later, colder, windier as I stomp on back home. When I turn onto the block, a police car is coming down. He sees me, stops…and backs up.

***

☞ **ADDRESSEE UNKNOWN.**

☞ **RETURN TO SENDER.**

☞ **POSTAGE DUE.**

Carved into the thick varnish which coats the graffiti scars in the elevator is a fresh deep inscription:

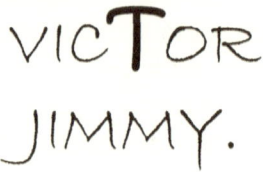

A message. They're with me. Only Judy calls me "Jimmy." Maybe the bent-top "T" means something. Maybe I think I know what to do.

OK. Here goes. Several of the apartment mailboxes have had their doors removed for replacement: maybe I'm supposed to put everything, and symbolically myself, into the mail. So I get the empty beer and Vienna sausage cans from outside my apartment and stick them in the mailbox openings, along with my *Daily News* and a ballpoint. Then I crumple my pack of Pall Malls with just a few smokes left and stick that in. I drape my overcoat over a corner and start to take off my shirt, shoes, and socks. Then a fella storms out of a lobby apartment.

"WHAT ARE YOU DOING HERE? WHAT ARE YOU PUTTING THAT STUFF IN THERE FOR? DON'T TAKE YOUR CLOTHES OFF IN HERE! WHAT'S THE MATTER WITH YOU? TAKE YOUR STUFF AND GET OUTTA HERE RIGHT NOW! HERE'S A DOLLAR. GO AND RIDE THE SUBWAYS!"

He hands me a buck and his voice drops. "Sorry I had to yell: that's for the benefit of the other tenants. You're supposed to be an intelligent man: you know I don't mean for you to go and ride the subways. Go and get your things back."

<<WHA?>> "Hey, thanks, man."

"By the way, one other thing. I was in the Navy — the *peacetime* Navy. You're supposed to be an intelligent man. You know you shouldn't be wearing that patch."

<<WHA?>> "Sorry. It's my father's shirt. He gave it to me. I didn't know." Blue-and-white cog 4th Service Command insignia on my left shoulder. The shirt was WWII U.S.A. khaki twill, custom-tailored, tapered, fit like starched skin, looked great with a solid navy tie. "Hey, I 'preciate your help. Sorry about the mess." I pull on my shoes and socks and stuff everything else into my overcoat pockets. "I'll get outta here right now and go catch a train."

Late at night the subway station escalator stops running, so I walk up the wooden steps, but a fella starts coming down — black guy, shiny hard black leather overcoat, carved ebony African totemic walking stick. "Hey, man, you got a smoke?"

I take out my pack of broken Pall Malls. "All I got is some butts, but you're welcome to one if you'd like."

"Hey, I better light yours first." It's good for a snatch of deep craving puffs. Then I buy two tokens and climb the stairs to the downtown platform. Could be a long wait for a train at this hour.

There's the guy with the shillelagh again. He pounds the stick on the platform planks once, twice, and a train starts out of the hole at 137th Street.

I take a seat on the train. The black-stick man stands at the pole in front of me. A few stops down the way, a TA cop comes through, gives him a high five and a handshake.

So I guess I have to go to the main post office. I could get off at Broadway and 34th, but they kept me running around enough, now they can wait a little bit. I take the long way around, past 34th all the way down through South Ferry and back up to Herald Square.

I follow some likely people off the train and ask them which way is the General Post Office. They only babble. I look up the P.O. phone number, but the public phones in the station are dead: no dial tone, even though that's supposed to be automatic for emergency calls. But of course. Telephones are competition.

Besides, do I really need directions? I oughta know my way around here. My $80 Panasonic® black-and-white TV and $65 algae-green London Fog® raincoat came from Macy's, World's Largest Store. My mother used to claim that Herald Square's landmark animated clock, Minerva and the Bellringers, was named after her. My grandfather had the Christmas kiddie ride concessions at one of the department stores in the district. I have seen the Parade and the movie at least a dozen times.

Just keep the Empire State Building at your back and you're going in the right direction.

Out of the subway I come up onto a side street. The Empire State topping is dark, or the view is fogged or blocked, and I am not sure whether I am heading east or west, north or south, or which way is which, when down the street right at me rushes this red-white-and-blue trailer truck marked "U.S. MAIL" in Federal Gold.

***

10001

"NEITHER SNOW NOR RAIN NOR HEAT NOR GLOOM OF NIGHT STAYS THESE COURIERS FROM THE SWIFT COMPLETION OF THEIR APPOINTED ROUNDS."

Herodotus, set full measure across the pediment all the way up 8th Avenue from W. 33rd to W. 34th Streets. Flanking, panels citing Cyrus the Great, Augustus Caesar, Cardinal de Richelieu, Mazarin. One brass handrail, centered up the long, shallow-pitched stairs to one lighted polished brass door.

These couriers. These *letters.*

The Miracle on 34th Street!

I walk up into a room a clearspan city block long, several stories high, nearly all dark. There is a giant-size guard packing a heavyweight pistol, and I ask him where I can find out about some property I dropped into a mailbox. He shows me to a barred frosted wire-glassed window off in a corner, where I have to squat down to tell my story through the small opening at the bottom. Then somebody directs me to the next window, which they raise open — "Now you can talk to us standing up."

They have to make some calls to find out what's where, so I get to wait and walk around, every measured step on the stone floor drumbeaten through the volume of the room.

Over one of the service windows is a sign:

<<Aha.>>

Of course I had to read the FBI MOST WANTED posters. <<Waitaminnit. I know this fella. J.J. Jacobs, from Spanish class,

usually slept in the back. Good picture. Easy-going OK guy, as I recall. Taking Spanish, he said, because that would be the native tongue of the next war. Reputedly a puke's jock: an activist who really acted. Wanted for destruction of federal property, conspiracy, flight to avoid prosecution, aggravated aggravation…. Yeah. He's been busy.>>

At a writing desk I see a receptacle marked "WASTE MATTER," where I get to dispose of the *Daily News,* Schaefer beer and New Iberia Vienna sausage cans, and other debris from my overcoat pockets. Several desks away is a guy with glasses, stubbly grubby beard, army field jacket. He walks past me and announces, "I'L DE-CON-*FUSE* THEM."

<<I could swear that voice was Pete Seeger. Holy shit.>>

At each end of the building I enter a silo-sized cylinder of armor-gauge black metal plates — all around and away up, the names of post office people who died in the wars.

<< "God damn! Well I declare! Have you seen the like?/ Their walls are built of cannonballs, their motto is 'Don't tread on me.'" The Grateful Dead, "Uncle John's Band.">>

The guard says they want to see me at the window. They say they think they have my stuff, but just to be sure, which particular corner was the mailbox on?

"Uhhh, Broadway and Tiemann, uh, north-, uh…." Then someone behind the window says "He ought to know where his extension is." <<WHA?>> To which I quip, "I guess we all ride the same trains" — not needed, not useful, not smart. They tell me to go back to the 125th Street branch and ask at the employees' entrance.

Out the front door and down the long stairs, turning once to take in the full breadth of the building and the grand expanse of the inscription. "You're mine now. Gotcha. I did it." Front and center out on the street, an idling truck, the only vehicle in sight, pulled away smartly. Down again in the subway — I did have a prepaid round trip — a train comes in minutes. What else did I expect?

Up in back of the 125th Street Post Office, where I had skulked and skedaddled just hours ago, I announce that they sent me from the General Post Office downtown, and I demand "mah proppitty back." Guard said they called him, but he has to make sure: "What's your name again?"

"Wisniewski. W...I...S...N...I...E...W...S...K...I."

"WISENIWESKI. Wizinski. Wizewski."

"W...I...S...N...I...E...W...S...K...I. *Wisniewski.*"

"Awright. Whatever. How much money was in the wallet?"

"Not sure exactly. Maybe $17."

"Can you describe your keys?"

"Keychain has a little cigarette lighter, size of your thumb, with a shield that says 'Outer Banks' and a picture of a sailing ship on it. Enamel picture. Lighter needs fluid. Souvenir. My sister gave it to me."

"Wait here." He turns to go inside and I see he is wearing an S&W Chief's Special snub-nose .38 at the small of his back. He brings out an envelope with the keys and wallet (turned out I had $67.00) and a form for me to sign. I thank him for his trouble, adding something like "I better get outta here before the troops follow."

Not needed, not useful, not smart. When am I gonna learn to shut up?

(Back down the street, a flock of Chinese guys walk past talking excitedly all at once. I didn't know it then, but that was a rattletrap, the first of many.)

Mission accomplished. But first things first. I need cigarettes and a beer and something to eat. By now it is like 4 a.m. or later, but there are a couple of all-night produce stand markets at 110th and Broadway, so I take a nice healthy walk, feeling stronger every step of the way. Then home with a six-pack of Bud, two packs of smokes — Maryland®, with the Made-For-Menthol™ blend, plus the standard red Pall Malls — and a big bag of Lay's® potato chips. Balanced breakfast.

As I get off the elevator on my floor, Karl Miller, the super's adopted son and suspected (later reportedly convicted, incarcerated in Attica) burglar-in-residence, wakes up from his post on the stairway leading up to the roof.

"Morning, Karl."

"Damn."

[As a breakthrough in burgling, Karl's technique is worth a sidebar. These apartments were typically secured by window grates, which at best took a little hard prying to bend open, and window glass, the best integral audible burglar alarm around, as well as the

63

potentially high visibility, not to mention precarious risk, of anyone out on the fire escapes. Doors featured the standard ordinary latch and deadbolt, which could be popped or picked with minimal skill and low-tech tools.

[The main protection was the Fox Police® Lock — not just among the most apt brand names ever coined, but ingeniously elegant, simple, and strong. The Police Lock operated with a carbon steel bar fitted in a brass floor plate and extending up at a 60° angle to a cast metal box mounted on the door. Unlocked, the bar moved freely. Turning the key moved the bar to trap it tightly in the box — for a formidable and all but unshakable brace on the door. Not only was the Police Lock cylinder hard to pick, but the resistance of the bar reinforced the integrity of the other locks.

[Of course, a fireman's halligan tool could split open the door frame, and the center panel was thin and lightweight to allow fast emergency access with a crowbar or an axe. But cops and firefighters were allowed to splinter wood and make noise. Burglars weren't.

[To defeat the Police Lock, Karl employed an accomplice: a gerbil. Yes. A *gerbil*. I am not making that up. A gerbil, which could be introduced into the target apartment under a security grate or through a quick, neat, 5" x 7" hole cut through window glass. The critter was trained to head straight for the base of the Police Lock bar and nudge it out of the braced position. Then, Karl could undo the other locks (if they were even locked at all: many people considered the Police Lock protection enough), achieve entry, heist the requisite TV, radio, or other small appliance (on the West Side uptown, residents had just a certain few items worth taking), and exit, stowing the swag on the roof for later retrieval if necessary. High speed, low risk: the 2-6 ranked B&E one notch above barking dog complaints.

[I had been burgled once, and all the circumstances pointed to an inside job. I figured then that the entry was conventional — 5" x 7" hole in bathroom window, and then they (why is it always "they"?) undid the window lock or pried it open and made off with a portable TV and portable typewriter. Cops showed up after three calls to the precinct, took the report and meandered around for all of maybe 5 minutes. "Officer, aren't you gonna check for fingerprints or like that?"

"You have a murder here?"

"Not that I know of. Not since I've been here, and the previous tenant didn't mention anything."

"When you have a murder, then we check for fingerprints."

"Oh."

"We'll let you know if your property turns up."

"You think it might be recovered?"

"Anything's possible. Don't count on it. Are you insured?"

"Just life insurance and Blue Cross. Guess that's only for murders too."

"Don't take it personal. These things happen."

"Yeah, I guess. OK, officers, thanks for your trouble."

[Then one evening I am startled by this brown furry longtailed shape sprinting through the living room. Aww, shit. What's a rat doing up on the 6th floor? Roaches I can put up with. Not rats. So after a few more fuzzy streak sightings, I ask Hector at the hardware store to show me a mousetrap, *para un ratoncito poquito.* The first trap he got out couldn't handle my cockroaches; the second might be fine for a white lab rat (which itself would be no match for my cockroaches.)

["*¿Cual es su mas grande matar los ratones?*" Hector brings out a slab of pine imprinted with the brand "VICTOR" and fitted with an auto-suspension-type coil spring and rebar gauge snapper.

"Yeah. That looks like the right size. I'll take it."

"You don' gotta mouse. You gotta *elephant.*"]

Meantime: I have a beer, chips, and smokes for breakfast. For dramatic effect, I pull on a grey hooded sweatshirt over my shirt and tie. To make a statement, although heaven knows what, I also take my blue SSCandB employee ID card out of my wallet and slap it down on top of the refrigerator.

The elevator comes up. On the car's linoleum floor is my copy of the Sunday New York *Times,* which Karl must have borrowed to read during his stakeout. It also came to mind that on the (*sans*) TV table there was a copy of a letter to my father describing my meeting with the Chairman of the Board, noting that "Heagan is a sentimental old coot," and closing with the line "Watch the papers." Karl did. Atop the neatly refolded *Times*, he left a note:

Dear Ling:
Victimized & Exhausted...,

which went on in this fashion for ten or fifteen lines filling the outside of a manila envelope. Ling, huh? I skimmed the note but did not recollect anything further at all at anytime thereafter. I still wonder if there might have been something there that I missed, that might have explained something, since everything was about to become downright inexplicable.

Watch the papers.

***

Business Reply Card

I get on the train for work fairly early, 7:30 a.m. or so, not having slept but having won.   At the first stop, the 116$^{\underline{th}}$ Street/Columbia University station, the car doors open and I hear a radio from the newsstand on the platform — George Harrison, "My Sweet Lord":

I really wanna see you, I really wanna see you,
I really wanna see you but it takes so long....

Then again at 96$^{\underline{th}}$ Street:

I really wanna see you, I really wanna see you

so I decide to stay on the local instead of changing to the express across the platform.   Once more at 59$^{\underline{th}}$ Street, again from the platform:

I really wanna see you but it takes so long, My Lord
(Hallelujah) (Hare Krishna) ....

Crosstown to Grand Central for the Lexington Avenue train to go just 9 blocks up to work, the next local stop. In the station there is an unusually loud and clear P.A. announcement: next train on the local track will be an express, which would take me up out of my way to 59th Street, so I want to let it pass. But as the express arrives, a crisply pretty blue-lidded blonde nudges her shoulder sharply into my arm.

OK. I get the idea. Express myself. Up at about 59th Street was that black building with the bright light on last night, where I expected Judy Appleton worked. I understand, Judy. I really wanna see you too. So I ride up and walk the eight blocks back down. I trust you saw that.

Today I am not the first person on our floor or in our bay. There are lights on in Cy Nathan's office, so I politely stick my head in, holding back what could have been the best line of the day: "Why, it's good old reliable Nathan," from *Guys and Dolls,* "The Oldest Established Permanent Floating Crap Game in New York." At least the song title was about to become highly meaningful.

[SFX: "TICKTICKticktickTickTickTICKETYTICK" —   Cy's collection of 20 or 30 antique clocks ratcheting up and under.]

"'Scuse me, sir, but was there some kinda problem or something here last night?"

"Well, Jim, we were robbed. Same thing happened about a year ago. And both times, it was a professional job."

<<HUH?>>

("Professional" was Cy's highest praise, but I couldn't figure out the "robbed" part. Maybe somebody just stole me from them. But what about a year ago? Nobody ever said anything about a robbery, actual or metaphorical. I only swiped some prototype cookie packages, oh, and some hot headshots. Can't be that.)

Cy asked if anything happened to me.

"Ahhh, had some hassles on the subway and around town, but everything's taken care of."

"Glad it worked out. Good to see you in."

"They don't call me 'Jimmy' for nothin'."

[SFX: "TICKTICKticktickTickTickTICKETYTICK" up and out]

Out my window that very bright light is still shining in the black skyscraper, the *2001* monolith, Tycho Magnetic Anomaly I.

[TMA. "It's a buckdancer's choice, my friend, better Take My Advice." — again The Dead.]

Not long before lunch Leo Keegan, Sunshine Biscuits account super, comes by the door and does a kind of striptease with a flapped piece of artwork, lifting the flap, grinning knowingly and flashing a big line art map of California. "Who can I get to mount this?" he wants to know, knowing very well whom.

California, eh? I could live with that. Had enough winter last night to last the year anyway.

Then I am talking to Vinnie, and we overhear Doc calling back to no one in particular, "We'll be by to pick up our prize package — after lunch." Several people echo "After lunch...after lunch." And Vinnie says, "That must mean you. Just stick a stamp to yourself, Jim. Stick a stamp to yourself, find the nearest mailbox and they'll pick you up. After lunch."

***

Writer's block, buster

The nearest mailboxes are on the corner right across the street. The light changes and I am ready to cross and SPLAT! — a corner-sized arc of greenish sheet ice lands at $51^{\underline{st}}$ and Lex, just a yard to my right. <<WHOA! Whazzat?>>

Behind me I hear someone say "That's far enough!"

I execute a quick left face and start walking down E. $51^{\underline{st}}$ to the next corner. Square in the middle of the block, sirens yowl: Engine 8 and Ladder 2, Seagrave 100' Rear Admiral, "Pride of Midtown," lunge out of their station right in front of me and stop hard at the curb, blocking the sidewalk at the firehouse entrance.

Voice behind me: "That's wide enough!"

I skitter across the street and down the block to stand at the mailboxes in front of the Summit Hotel, but the doorman comes out and yells "Girlfriend overseas!" Somehow I get the idea I shouldn't be on this corner, either. So I beat it down the street and end up on the other side of Lexington, where several girls from the Cathedral High School are singing Christmas carols, loudly, badly, weeks late.

One says, in a nearly nasty pubescent whine, "Now we're a sex trap."

Another voice behind me pronounces, "That's *broad* enough."

Then I am about to cross $51^{\underline{st}}$ and Lex again, this time on the other side, and SPLAT! — another slab of greenish ice lands smack in front of me.

<<Wha? Ice from the sky. Wow. OK. Got it. I'm not supposed to cross my block. Better not look up, either. Jeez.>>

<< Now I get it. Crossing the block thus — ✛ — puts crosshairs on it and a bomb falls. >>

As I sidestep, not sure which way to head, I hear "He's got time on his hands!" Oh. Gotcha. Sure. How silly of me. They want a symbolic gesture. I stop at a mailbox and toss in my new stainless steel Timex Christmas present wristwatch.

"That's long enough!"

I think I better just go for a walk. Too much heat around here.

On a side street I find myself walled in by a load of office furniture, and blocked by an old brown Ford pickup, backing up slowly over the sidewalk into a delivery entrance. Nowhere to go but

back behind that truck. I see the hand-painted lettering on the cab
door:

FRIENDS' MEETING HOUSE
Someplace, L.I., N.Y.

Must be my ride. They said they were gonna pick me up. So I
vault over the tailgate into the canvas-draped cargo bed.

The driver comes back and asks what I'm doing.

"You backed me up, man. I'm a Quaker."

"Hey, look, pal, I gotta work in the city."

"Yeah, well. I'm lookin' for a job in the country." Hopped out
and hit the street. "Hey man. Never saw ya."

Barely a few steps further on a U.S. Mail truck horses up onto the
sidewalk. I don't jump in here, because they usually have a sign that
says "NO RIDERS," which is what I think the driver is pointing to on
the dashboard, but the sign says

LOOK BEFORE BACKING

Waitaminnit. So *this* is what it's all about. "LOOK BEFORE
BACKING." OK. Now I get it.

["**LOOK BEFORE BACKING**." I remembered Karl Miller's
note of this morning: "Dear Ling," and a story in *FORTUNE*.
"LOOK BEFORE BACKING" was James J. Ling's corporate
formula. The great conglomerateur said he simplified his business
philosophy and operating principles to universals that anyone could
understand. Nobody could ever complain that the rules were too
complicated. If you could drive a car, open a door, light a match, or
even use a toilet, you perforce had a complete working knowledge of
the rules in practice.

These were basics, not B-school:

CROSS YOUR BLOCK
SET YOUR TRAP
BACK UP, BACK DOWN
PUSH/PULL
NO U-TURNS.

Above all,

NEVER CROSS THE BIG T,

whatever that meant. And always,

"TAKE CARE."

[That phrase was starting to tag onto the end of certain people's conversations, like *"Ciao"* or "Peace" or "Keep the faith." Take care of what? Be careful? Perhaps to the uninitiated. The expanded, decrypted meaning:

TAKE CARE OF THE BIG SECRET,

whatever that might be. Thus the antiphon, as two people part ways.

"TAKE CARE." "YOU BET."[*]

$\leftarrow T \text{-------} T \rightarrow . \quad T \text{------} T.$

And the Big Secret drops between them.

[O my. I just found out the Big Secret or at least a fairly Big Secret, and I already knew the Pretty Big Secret. The U.S. Post Office was about to be privatized, and Ling-Temco-Vought was going to run it.

[So that's where Judy Appleton works, up in that black monolith. Judy got a job with L-T-V. So that's why she wouldn't say where she worked. So that's why Cy said we were robbed. I just got pirated by Ling-Temco-Vought.]

Some lunchers pass by and behind me I hear "Jumped right in!" "Just like in a *cab!*" They noticed. Straight ahead, an empty tank truck bounces and clangs down Second Avenue. A rattletrap. Alright. Fine. Big black mark next to my name. I better not plan on becoming chairman of L-T-V. Then a fella comes by pulling on his gloves and giving me the "Hook 'em horns" two-finger salute.

***

---

[*] I recall hearing the combo for the first time as an exchange between Bill Timm and Bill Weithas, getting out of a cab in front of the office and holding the door open for me as I scooted off to the airport one afternoon that past summer.

Slaughter on Park Avenue

The lunchtime maelstrom takes me around and about, with no destination. I go with the flow to the south side of the New York Central Building, the rococo tower standing athwart Park Avenue, the anchor of the Superblock. A door is held open and I go in.

I am dazzled. This is not a lobby. This is a palace. This is a basilica. This is all polished marble and metal, travertine and jaspé arches opening to elevators gilded outside, crimson and sky blue enameled within, luminaires like baroque pearls above, and ahead, through crystals set in wrought iron intricacies, all of Park Avenue in the fulness of the midday light shining from here up to the horizon.

"Yo!" I hear a guard sound off.

Oops. Uh-oh. Intruder alert. Shoulda used one of the open-air pedestrian arcades on either side. So I scrunch and slink, neck in, head down, shoulders curled, knees bent, in defilade among a procession of tall men in homburgs and charcoal Chesterfields, through the lobby and out another door held open to the sidewalk, square at the centerline of Park Avenue.

Right in front, an aluminum-leaf silver Studebaker Hawk, window glass tinted green black, pulls up and stops. Man in sunglasses riding shotgun opens, glares, and then slams the door. Uh-oh. Let's take a walk around the block.

Around and around and over and across. Somehow, following a running relay of neoclassic collector cars, I end up down in front of the U.N. Thence, I am in a narrow sunless skyless blind alley behind the J.P. Morgan Post Office Substation. There is a heavy delivery van built of brushed cold-rolled steel plate with bold black graffiti across the back doors:

GREENWICH VILLAGE PEACE BUS

CRUSH CAPITALISM.

Uh-oh. These people don't fool around.

I pass a stunning six-foot woman who hands me a leaflet for some porn house and points a direction with a flick of her eyes and head. OK. They went thataway. So do I.

Down a side street runs a continuous chrome yellow line of cabs, one in the middle fast-flashing his rear-window-mounted backup lights. I thought this was just traffic, or a flicker of recognition from a cabbie to a old fare and overtipper. Never occurred to me that he meant for *me* to back up, until the street ended on Park Avenue. Then another '50s classic car came by, door opened and slammed. Let's take a walk around the block. Right behind, dry hopper truck barrels down Park. Another rattletrap.

I remembered a line from *New York* Magazine: "When Jim Ling's cabs hit the city...." Flocks, packs, prides, herds of cars of all kinds, uncommon makes and models, Packard, DeSoto, Ford Ranchero, batwing Chevy, fatso Caddy, all with opaque tinted glass, every one pristine.

Once I get off the Superblock, there is another tall striking woman in fur handing out leaflets — "United Mutual Savings Bank." As I take one she catches my eye and motions me left with a sharp nod. Gotcha.

A phalanx of swinging doors opens from inside all at once in close order drill. PUSH. The next row in reverse. PULL. Then again. And again.

I get led around back onto Park, straight at a street sign:

> # NO
> ## COMMERCIAL
> ## TRAFFIC

Yeah. OK. Hey, wait. I'm not commercial. Oh. Well, yeah, maybe. Maybe I am in a sense.

Whoa. That sign just moved higher. That signpost just telescoped up.

The same sign is on every block, both sides — "*NO* COMMERCIAL TRAFFIC." "NO *COMMERCIAL* TRAFFIC."

But I swear the positions keep changing. (The *New York* article mentioned reports of signposts going up and down. First the subways run on command, now this. Must be a master control somewhere with a lot of switches.)

"NO COMMERCIAL TRAFFIC." So what does it mean anyway? No Agency correspondence through the mails? No freebie franking? No self-promotion or self-aggrandizement or exploitation — something like that. Quasi-public, not semi-private. Whatever it is, I get the message.

Rattletraps jangling every time I turn around: cement mixer, bulk carrier, dump truck, flatbed, masonry truck with bricks or cement blocks and an onboard clanking crane. Addresses lettered on the sides — Butler Street, Fisk Street, Penn Avenue — names from my old neighborhood.

From perfect strangers, perfect people in passing in velvet-collared overcoats, homburgs ("brass hats") or brimless V-crowns or crumply helmetic hemispheres or flat fur[*] headgear, lines loud and clear:

"PITTSBURGH, I THINK"
"THEREFORE...YOU LOSE."
"THAT'S A GREAT IDEA!"
"THAT'S THAT."
"CAN'T SAY."
"THIS IS TRUE."
"TAKE CARE." "YOU BET."
"TAKE CARE OF YOURSELF."
"TAKE CARE NOW." "YOU TOO."
"TAKE IT EASY."

A final visual statement: two men with pipes blow cumulus puffs:
"PUT *THAT IN* YOUR PIPE AND SMOKE IT."

I get the point. These are the rules. This is who we are and how we do things. We have you surrounded. We are thousands of people and countless cars and places and things and power you never

---

[*] The hat shapes seemed to signify rank — flat, helmet, V, homburg in ascending order. (My maternal grandfather and Monsignor Sliwinski from the old Polish parish wore homburgs.) The Chesterfield was evidently reserved for mid-level to senior people. For travel, standard uniform, enabling recognition as needed: white shirt, thin black tie, so I think I once heard.

imagined.   We have shown this to you because we know you're a smartass who doesn't impress easily, but you'd better appreciate who and what you're dealing with.

It worked. I had no idea what to expect, not even after last night. I certainly never expected *this*. I had been up and down and around all those blocks many times before and never seen the like. Unanticipated, unprecedented, out-and-out unbelievable.   But very convincing, especially to someone sometimes scared of his own shadow — and humbling to ego and arrogance that had been solid brass and bravado.

Back at the shop, I tell Vinnie, "Kinda rough out there."

"They don't fool around with someone with hair on his face," he said as he stroked his goatee. Right. I had a day's worth of stubble.

Bill Timm, the personnel VP, calls me down to his office late in the afternoon. I think we are talking in L-T-V-ish, such as I heard over lunch, and which I figure means speaking in all caps and watching "T" words.   Bill asks if I am feeling alright, wonders if maybe I have been working too hard, suggests that I take a few days off.

I allow as to how I have never felt better, but I will think about taking some time. For whatever reason, he worries aloud about what would happen if I ended up in The Tombs.

<<WHA?>>   I'm tempted to respond, "Sullivan Law's all they can prove" — carrying a piece without a license — which is all one is supposed to admit to fellow prisoners in a holding cell. But the Agency's first name is "Sullivan," and it might seem disrespectful. No more Mr. Smartass. No sir. Then, whatever for, he asks if I'm religious.   I swipe a line from another copywriter, the indomitable John Lyons, and offer that I'm a Catholic trying to be a Christian. On Bill's desk is a conspicuous copy of the magazine *Airline Management,* buckslip addressed to "Hal Dover." No such person.

Back in my office I begin to wonder. How can you cross the Big T anyway? With the arc of the crosspiece, you'd slide off. And there is really not one single Big T. First I thought it ran from the TIME-LIFE Building to the L.A. *Times* Tower, if they had one. I also envisioned a continuous transcontinental series, like transmission towers — T T T T T. Or the 2D T was a cross-section of a 3D umbrella. Or right in the middle there was a hole one could fall

75

through. Then it occurred to me that there was a fateful way to cross the Big T, that is, sagittally, with an ICBM arcing across from over the Pole. That would make the graffito come true:

CRUSH CAPITALISM.

Or did that  symbol mean that when the conglomerates glommed enough to achieve a critical mass, that fascism would crush capitalism?

Whoever and whatever they were or it was, they could pulverize my heretofore crushproof self like so much foamy furnace slag. Of course, Clients can do that readily to agencies and agency people. Maybe they just wanted to dramatize that to me. The exercise at lunch could have been just a large-scale demo as a graphic reminder. Point taken. Message received. But really — who are they trying to impress? Me? Whatever for? Hey, I just work here.

Something is obviously, audibly afoot. Outside my office I overhear Jack Thwaites announcing "Project titled: 'Put A Man On The Moon.'" Vinnie says "Charlie has this friend named Gretchen....", and past the corner of my eye flashes this Valkyriean blonde, looking a lot like the model who lives directly across the airshaft from my apartment.

At the end of the day, several folks announce that they're going to stop for a drink "at Junior's." Whatever. I'll just wait. Then a familiar noise, but way out of place — paper bag with empty cans rattling, sounding like Alex picking up my rubbish in the morning. I'll wait and see.

The bright light still burned up in the black tower.

***

Night vision

After dark I lit the fat candle that I sometimes burned on my windowsill, tonight a light to meet the light uptown, and invoked the lines from *Mame*:

Because we need a little Christmas, right this very minute,

Candles in the window, carols at the spinet....

I sat at my desk and stared out my window and watched the skyscrapers of the city light up with the pictures and things I had stuck on the walls of my apartment — all blown up, hanging hundreds of feet high over midtown Manhattan, *mirabile visu*, all across the night. All the breath in me came out in one "Wowwww!" Omigod. Lookit!

My Margaret Keane litho, three lady harlequins, done as three stick figures strung down one building. Profile of a boy, the Paul Davis-illustrated United Farm Workers' *Viva La Huelga* poster *chico* on a building alongside them. Hexagon framing a stick figure: poster of the Resurrection, POV inside the tomb looking out. East, the necklace lights of the 59th Street Bridge forming a cup, right where I kept mine. A $ sign — framed first dollar I ever earned — ten stories tall on another building. West, a Gronk, all square teeth and bugeyes and monster flattop, grinning down from a wall of windows. Further up, my profile, art-pad-size caricature by Old Mark, hung with pushpins in my bathroom and now displayed down here, on a scale of twenty stories or more — weak chin, receding hairline, squint and all, and — and exhaling smoke from the mouth and nostrils!

Wotta surprise! Wotta show! Thank you. To see and think better, I turned out all my office lights, with only the candle burning.

After some time Old Mark and Tiernan McBride, bearish Irish TV producer given to wearing love beads, came in behind me and asked if I was all right.

<<So they sent the Catholics to lead me along.>>

"I'm just watching this cartoon show. Look out there!"

"James, those are just people turning lights on and off," Tiernan said.

"Well of *course* they are."

"James, we just want to see if you're OK."

"Never better. I feel fine."

"I mean how are you mentally, James? Like how's your head? Really? You're not going to walk under a train or something tonight?"

"Of course not. Hey — what's going on here?"

"Did you know that some people are saying that the thing you did for Doc was an inside job? That your office belongs in a place that can be hosed down?"

"Wha?"

"That you do your best work in the bathroom?"

"Fuck that shit. What's going on here?"

"James, think you might want to wash your hands?"

Whatever. Snide was out of character for Tiernan, but everything had become utterly uncharacteristic now. I went down the hall to the bathroom, but there was a rubbish cart and a mop in front of the door. Back in, Tiernan was on a phone with no buttons lit, playing back "10th floor? Weithas's office?"

"Anything interesting in the bathroom, James?"

"I saw a trap and a block. Also notice that you were on a dead line."

"I think you may be needed downstairs."

So I went into the stairwell to go down. The door closed and locked behind me.

For each of five flights down, the doors were locked. Another prank. Shoulda expected it. Hosed down indeed: on the landing was a bracket with a length of 1½" line and brass nozzle tip.

At least they knew where to find me. I hollered some, banged on the doors and pipes, sat down by an ashtray under a placard reading "PLEASE," and having been up all the night before, then run all around town, fell fast asleep.

"What are you doin' in here?" I awoke to look up at a couple of building security guards and a squad of cops.

"I work here. Somebody locked me in."

"Sure they did. Let's see your arms, Pockets. You a junkie?"

I pulled up the sleeves on my sweatshirt. "Naw, hey, I'm clean."

"You got any I.D.?"

SSCandB employee I.D. card was back home on the refrigerator. "Forgot my Agency I.D."

"Well, you can't sleep in the stairwell."

"I didn't plan to. Somebody locked me in here."

"You locked yourself in."

"Whatever. Lemme just go to my office and get my overcoat."

This prank is getting pretty drawn out, but I'll play along. Not much else I can do.

Back onto the 15th floor, I took the lead and turned on all the lights without looking for the switches, a skill acquired by frequent first-in morning arrivals. Behind me a guard or cop said, "He knows where all the lights are." Yeah. Sly inside-job burglar's trick. Jeez. After I got my coat, the senior guard said, "We'll just tell your bosses that you had one too many." On the way out and down in the elevator, I checked out the NYPD contingent. Male model faces and immaculate uniforms, sharp even for the 1-7, the Silk Stocking district, the most fashionable precinct in town. They didn't look anything like cops. They hadn't frisked me, hadn't cuffed me, hadn't even asked my name or taken a report. Somehow, after the past 24 hours, the extraordinary was expected S.O.P. The party was probably uptown.

In the 51st Street subway station, I crossed my block and bought a symbolic bag of peanuts ("I always thirst after salted peanuts") from a vending machine. Rattletrap trash train came through, followed by the Lex local. At Grand Central, on the floor at the foot of the stairs to the crosstown Flushing train, the front page of the *Daily News*:

PLOT TO KIDNAP
HENRY KISSINGER
Berrigans[*] sought

In passing, I heard "He sees the same thing every day."

The IRT 7th Avenue uptown, grimed outside but polished and perfect within, not the regular everyday rolling stock, ran like an electric rocket sled on continuous welded rail. A Chance Vought aircraft. (Instead of "I'll catch a train," I thought, "I'll take a Chance.") As the train pulled out of the ground and up the ramp to

---

[*] Marginal connection at best. Vinnie mentioned either Dan or Phil as a teacher or classmate, and one or the other crashed with my (lower-quality) dope dealer while on the lam. Also in my wallet I carried a card: "I AM AN IMPORTANT CATHOLIC. In Case of Accident, Get Me A Bishop. Or at least a Jesuit."

the Manhattan Valley trestle, alongside ran a bullet-nosed Mack fire engine, flashing lights and flying American flags on the cab, but these flags carried peace symbols surprinted on the blue field.

Back home, no party. Worse, no beer in the house, so down to the all-night market. On the return train, I picked up a discarded *Daily News* and read that Father Dan (or Phil) had been arrested amid protests of his innocence by a Pakistani or Indian named Amahl, with some other details that sounded strangely familiar, but of course I was getting used to that.

Home again, I saw a neighbor, same guy who gave me the dollar, sliding "Empire Telephone Answering Service" leaflets under doors. When he spotted me, he winked and pulled an Arabesque scarf over his head. Aha. Amahl and the Night Visitors.

***

His Master's Voice

I opened a Bud, lit a Pall Mall, sat down and turned on the radio, WHN-AM, 1050 kHz. The news: the plot to kidnap Henry Kissinger...by an organization called The East Coast Conspiracy to Save Lives...found in suspect's quarters were images of Franklin D. Roosevelt <<bust of FDR on my desk>>, pens and pencils, cigarettes, glass-cutting instruments.

Other news: Super Bowl Weekend. <<Wait — that's next week.>> "The President has relaxed restrictions on the importation of foreign steel to the West Coast...." <<My United States Steel chrome coil spring pencil holder?>> "Vice President Humphrey...." <<Huh?>> Traffic: "Cars are traveling in packs." <<Seen that.>> Weather: "+20°F to -20°F." <<At altitude?>> "Precip probability: 'bout zip." <<Gotcha.>> "The phone company will pay all the bills." <<Bill Timm? Bill Weithas?>> "And that's valid." <<Among my favorite expressions>>. Then the WHN station ID jingle. "H-N TEN-FIFTY. *HEAR IT!*"[*]

<<The East Coast Conspiracy To Save Lives. They must need to get me out of here under cover of night. I envision a charter busload of people coming to take me to an isolated corner of JFK, where I will be loaded with my containerized belongings aboard a B747, mail-truck-liveried, white-red-and-blue, with "U.S. MAIL" in Federal Gold on the upper deck, Raymond Loewy's eagle logo on the tail, flight plan filed to LAX, maybe side trip to the Super Bowl.>>

<<WHN is indeed 1050 on the AM dial (my favorite station until reformatted from Broadway to crossover country), but this audio isn't broadcast. Personal narrowcast. Must be a carrier current setup, putting the signal through the building's wiring, maybe from a studio in the basement or across the courtyard.>>

Now that I had everything figured out, I laid back and listened as HN 1050 played an eclectic, didactic mix, Top 40/Oldies/Easy Listening/AOR/ MOR/C&W/....

---

[*] The radio. Of course. Naturally. What else? My generation grew up with AM (up, 'way up and under throughout) as our lives' soundtrack, oldies as milestones, jingles as motets, folk rock as battle hymns.

♫ A Perry Como medley (ANNCR: Listen closely: one of these songs will tell you where you're going):

♪ "Find A Ring", which the Agency (freely) adapted as the jingle for Ballantine Beer with its Venn diagram pretzelian logo:
Take a ring, and add another ring, and another ring...
And now it's pree-mi-umm, it's a very special glass of beer!

♪ "Catch A Falling Star," no resemblance to the Donne poem, little relevance to the personal situation except melodramatically;

♪ "Seattle," <<*Seattle?*>> (ANNCR: And we don't have to tell you what TV show that's from) << *"Here Come The Brides"*>> <<!?!>> —
The bluest skies you've ever seen are in Seattle,
And the hills the greenest green in Seattle....

<<*SEATTLE?*>>

♫ "Beautiful People," Melanie, rock candy, refined sucrose:

Beautiful people,
You ride the same subway as I do every morning...

♫ "Watching Scotty Grow," Bobby Goldsboro:

There he sits with a pen and a yellow pad.
"BRLFQ" spells "Mom and Dad" ....

<<OK, so my handwriting's illegible.>>

♫ The Gospel:

♪ "Amazing Grace," Judy Collins and bagpipes;

♪ "Flesh and Blood," Johnny Cash;

♪ "Who Will Answer?", Ed Ames, *basso apocalypso* asking the eternal questions of the moment —

And if a secret button's pressed,
Because one man has been outguessed, who will answer?
[REVERB] Alleluia [CROSSFADE CHORAL], alleluia....

♪ "I Want Some Red Roses For A Blue Lady," Bobby Vinton, Mariolatry and matriarchy*;

♪ "Let It Be Me," The Four Freshmen (or Four Someones), I bless the day I found you, I wanna stay around you....

<<Waitaminnit. I found you. You didn't find me. I found *you.*>>

♫ Tony Orlando and Dawn's 2nd and 3rd Greatest Hits:

♪ "Candida" and

♪ "Knock Three Times (on the ceiling if you want me, twice on the pipe if you ain't gonna show)"

♫ Ballads of the Old West:

---

* In my wallet, the obligatory holy picture of the Blessed Virgin Mary from my mother's funeral. For Mother's Days, birthdays, and hospitalizations, I invariably sent her roses, not out of extravagance but because I knew nothing much about flowers.

"Git Along, Little Dogies"

(ANNCR: For a cowboy who won't be riding the rails any more);

 "Reuben James," Kenny Rogers and The First Edition or Whoever —

Reuben James[*], you were the sheriff of Madison County town,
Silver hair, furrowed brow, callused hand upon the plow....

Meantime I snacked and smoked and sipped beer and coffee, reveling in my own private radio program. But what did I expect?
And thence, the finale:

 "Turn Around, Look At Me," The Vogues:

...There is someone watching your footsteps,
Turn around, look at me....
<<I preferred the novelty parody by Frank Gorshin (star of the open-and-shut musical *Jimmy!*, a *nuovo-Fiorello!* about Mayor Walker), with impressions inserted in the lyric — Richard Burton, Dean Martin, Lee Marvin: "Yeah, well, you turn around and I'll paint your wagon.">>

 Tom Jones,

There goes my only possession; there goes my everything,

synched with the heavy metal bass line of the IRT 7th Avenue local literally up, over; and out;

 "We've Only Just Begun," The Carpenters;

---

[*] Had to be Judy Appleton's special request, as I once took her to Reuben's Deli, believing it to be kosher to comply with her religious practices, but of course it wasn't, except for the vegetable plate...and she knew my right index finger grew a thick oval callus with heavy typing.

"Goodnight My Love," The Four Ibids:

If you should awake in the still of the night, please have no fear, For I will be there, you know I care….

Reluctantly I went to bed.

***

Backing to basics

"H-N TEN-FIFTY. Hear it!"

"Now for the news. Cars are traveling in packs. People are advised to stay inside. Lunch will be at The Press Box."

<<Heard good things about that steakhouse. Waitaminnit. My (student) press card is right here on the dictionary stand by the chair.>>

"Dinner will be at The Sign of the Dove."

<<Old Mark touted that place for snowjob romantic dates. Waitaminnit. I have a mobile of doves (impulse cheapie from Azuma, either an artistic statement about peace or a kinetic image of local wildlife) hanging from the bedroom ceiling light.>>

"Your moving agent is John Gilhooley of North American Van Lines, Far Rockaway."

<< "Hey, Far Rockaway, don't pull the Doc away." — *Funny Girl*>>

Then evidently I was supposed to go in and take a nap. This soon got boring: I was restless and anxious to get the show on the road. I went back into the living room and the radio intoned: "HN 1050. For Traffic Headaches." Back to bed.

After some time the phone rang. "Jimmy, this is the Old Man."

(My father had *never* referred to himself that way. Nor did I, openly. In fact, in the old neighborhood parochial school, the nuns told us that referring to parents as "Old Man" or "Old Lady" was disrespectfully sinful.)

My father had heard from Bill Timm that I left a candle burning in my office window and was subsequently found asleep in a stairwell. <<Hold it now. I'm out one day, not even that, and the vice president, personnel, calls my family?>>

Stilted exchange. I'm being cryptic and sounds like he has a script. At least he said "Sounds like a put-up job to me." Then Dad said I should do one thing.

"What's that?"

"Drink."

(He would never say that. He objected to drinking and despised drinkers, in part because his office was two doors down from a tavern. Often enough during the winter a falling-down drunk would leave the

43$^{\underline{rd}}$ Street Bar, soft-shoe on the ice and snow, land hard on the pavement, then pick himself up and do a purposeful pratfall on the sidewalk outside the office, calculating that a dentist would have deeper-pocketed liability insurance than a beer garden, but not seeing that this sidewalk was scrupulously swept bare dry concrete, which occasionally had to be photographed with the family Ansco as evidence, most convincingly in the presence of the would-be victim.)

I genuinely expected that the next call would be in the voice of my deceased mother. They could do that. I could handle that. C'mon. Try it.

This must be a test, and more of a test than I had realized. A communications test, evidently, possibly involving responses more physical than answering the phone on the first ring. So I changed into a pair of sweatpants. Then the radio:

"You're gonna need more than two pair of pants for this. And by the way, those are the *hugliest* pantihose I've ever seen."

<<They can see in here. Thought so. So what? Probably right across the way.>>

The phone rang. "Is this Dr. Zimmerman?", in Kirk Bachler's muffled Minnesota accent.

"Uh, no, sorry, Kemo Mesabi." <<Can't be this easy.>>

***

I can relate what happened next, and how, but not easily why. What happened, so it came clear to me soon enough, I had read about years before in one of the Old Man's *macho* magazines, *True* or *Argosy.* This was "negative motivation," a training method utilized by elite units of the military, Rangers or Green Berets or whatever.

The trial was as much psychological and emotional as physical. There was a catch: the trainee always, invariably, inevitably fails. In the process, after extreme exertion, the subject seizes upon something and holds it as one's most precious possession. (A beer can pop top was the example I recalled.) But then he realizes failure, typically on a planted technicality. That moment is marked and the shame of the loss seared ineradicably with the sounding of a failure siren. You lost the mission or the platoon or the battle or the war.

I can describe what I did; the reason why was because I had to — and you had to be there. I gathered from the radio, the phone, voices in the hall and sounds in the building that I was supposed to do some exercise. "Knock three times on the ceiling if you want me, twice on the pipe if you ain't gonna show." Knock, knock, knock, back up; knock, knock, back down. Low crawl up from the bathroom door, through the bedroom and the French doors to the front, then back down. Up on the belly, down on the back.

Forearms, elbows and knees up, shoulders, buttocks, thighs and heels down, upping and backing, back and forth, until the apartment got dark and the brightest light was a slit in the front door jamb. By then I was backing with something to prove or something to settle, keeping on keeping on with exhortations from the hall and my grunting growling chanting "We're Number One! We're Number One! We're Number One!"

On one lap, almost all the way up through the darkness to the light, my hand found a piece of wood, a matchstick at most, and I held onto it like a sonofabitch.

I kept doing it doggedly. Then when I was on my back in the bathroom a strobe flashed somewhere up above and there was a sudden thought:

"What did the Old Man *say?*"

"LOOK BEFORE BACKING."

With that insight and outcome I could climb up in the chair, light a smoke, open a beer. He did say "Drink," after all. And no matter what he said, I hadn't eaten all day, so I grabbed some slices of Oscar Mayer pressed ham and bit mouthfuls right out of my fist. The radio started playing the theme from *Love Story.*

He didn't say "Eat." Before I had swallowed a bite — all the fire engine sirens on Morningside Heights started to scream from what seemed to be right up around the corner. The radio played Janis Joplin, "Take another little piece of my heart now, baby....", followed by The Carpenters, "We've Only Just Begun."

Only just begun.

***

Don Booth called the next morning and mentioned "our Little Action Project." Dropped in my lap, huh? Bill Timm called and repeated his suggestion that I take a few days off. The radio announced "a Bovril Break," and Mizz Swazey came in with her dog and a brace of beers. On later visits she would bring in miniatures or half-pints of Hennessey Cognac (Schieffelin & Co. Client product), which she said "the man in the liquor store paid for."

Regularly she also delivered gossip, guidance, proverbs, and parables. For instance, she had a sister in "Lexington, New York," in a house that had brass pipes; sometimes she said her sister was worried about me. She hinted that SSCandB held a second mortgage on the building; the first was held by the grand old firm of Bing & Bing, owners of Beekman Place, trustees of the heritage of Alexander M. Bing, the Helmsley and Trump of his day. Swazey said she remembered when 45 Tiemann was a luxury building and the site of the Grant Houses project was all pasture.

Thence back to backing. I was getting better at it, and, I thought, beginning to come to understand the reason behind the exercise. But night fell — Friday night — and the ordeal seemed endless and I panicked.

I hoisted an empty Coke bottle ("the emergency" from the 26th Precinct) up onto the shelf in the living room window.

The phone rang almost instantly. Cold call bolt out of the blue. Alan Magan, kid from my high school whom I might have seen in passing a few times in a few years, asked me to come over to his place on 122nd Street.

I could hardly see my way clear to get over there, since I was not wearing my glasses. This challenge started with the backing and would continue for the duration of the training, getting around the city legally half-blind — acuity 20/200 right, 20/100 left — ultimately learning to adjust and manage a handicap down to a merely (or depending on circumstances, highly) inconvenient impairment.

Jim Ling's cabs were out on Broadway, circling, blocking, leading. I had a Gallo Wine delivery truck to follow down. Then a VW Beetle with skis on the roof hustled across Broadway past the Jewish Theological Seminary to point the way to Alan's building. Skis indeed, but I saw where to go.

In Alan's lobby was a hand-lettered sign that said "**PERSONAL PSYCHOLOGY.**" I took that as a caution and a constraint. Upstairs, I was led to a seat on and in a velvet wrap-around pillow, then offered dope and apple juice. People were settling in, with more arriving. Out toward the door, I overheard "Nobody thought it would happen this soon." Also a greeting: "Alan Shepherd."

89

Alan's living room just about filled up with people. In the dim light and odd quiet I could only guess who was who, but everyone sorta looked somewhat like everyone I knew, including some only casual acquaintances, and several who must have gone well out of their way and gotten up here awfully fast.

Alan and I talked a little: I think I was properly circumspect, but unavoidably spilled a few beans. Why did I suspect that conversation was interrogation? Why did I worry that whatever I said slid secrets between the lines? Another overhearing: "Did you see any foreign cars around? He drives a foreign car. A Triumph, isn't it?"

I got ready to leave, get out and think. When I was out into the hall, I overheard:

"Did he drop anything?"

"Just this." Clinkclink. Alan knocked a key off the door lintel.

Just this. Just our back door key. Uh-oh. Then I thought, not only is Columbia somehow loosely connected to this training, maybe as a psychology or sociology study, but the people I know around here — everyone knows The Wizard — are somehow highly involved.

That's what's so remarkable: these are the unlikeliest people to be collaborating with the corporate system. Heaven forfend. Suits, even mine, made them nervous. Individual liberty and privacy mattered immeasurably more than the profit motive. Business was capable of wrongdoing. The power structure was not to be trusted. Who knows what these folk knew, or why they signed on, or if they sold me out, and for how much. The wondering that started then only kept widening and deepening.

"Take care," said Alan. He kicked his heel back against the door jamb.

"Er, you bet." At least I got the response right.

***

On the way back I followed various vehicles finally onto LaSalle Street, looked up and o God, looming lit up for thirty Gothic grey limestone stories, stern, menacing, fearsome and unforgiving, by God that building was malevolently looking down on me, the tower of Riverside Church. The Big T. Never cross it. Cross it and it falls on you. Cross it and get crushed. O Christ.

90

When I got home I looked into my mailbox and retrieved the new issue of *Esquire* — cover photo of Joe Namath on a motorcycle, from the current movie "C.C. and Company," alongside a stinging headline:

SISSY BARS WILL BE LOWER NEXT YEAR.

Once upstairs, slightly stoned and scared silly, I prostrated myself on the rug in the bedroom, and up from the courtyard came an *ersatz* Hebroid chant,

Yisraöl Mann, he's our Old Man, he's our Old Man

as the subway ground loud overhead.

After five or ten minutes of my prone abjection, Bob Martin called. Just as background: Bob came and went, here and there, now and then. Long ago he had set out to create and live his own lifestylistic, conspicuously and self-consciously autobiographical adventure. Back in that demonstrative era Bob stood out with the pioneering leadership of a newly emerging, none-too-popular cause. To me, gay rights constituted a logical subset of civil rights: my categorical imperative here was "Live and let live." To Bob, it was a crusade, from the foundation of the Student Homophile League (*née* the sheerly coincidentally but unfortunately abbreviated Columbia University Mattachine Society), and thence a quest, to Quakerism, which got him arrested at the White House and, in lieu of nominal bail, gang-banged on the same tier as G. Gordon Liddy in the D.C. Jail, to a test case for peeing in a North Carolina parking lot, to outing himself in the U.S. Navy ("Don't ask, don't tell, don't get an undesirable discharge"), to ordination as a Buddhist monk, to heaven-knows-where now. Back then, I hadn't heard from him in months or more, which was usual.

"Do you want to go to one of those singles places?", Bob asked over the phone. I assumed he meant one of his kind of places. Even if it were one of mine....

"Not quite up for that."

"I take it you'd sooner stay in."

"Much safer."

"Well, let me stop by."

"Couldn't hurt. I don't know what's happening here, Mr. Jones."

"We're off to see The Wizard."

So in he came wearing his sailor suit, right off stripping down to his T-shirt. I explained my predicament as best I could without stipulating facts. Then he asked, "Where are you heading?" Aha. Trick question. Course 090°. "East."

He told me about a great movie: "Little Big Man." Then, "For every action there is an equal and opposite reaction." Plus a line from Simon and Garfunkel: "Any way you look it at, you lose." His parting words: "Bleeding stops."

So that is why red lights are red.

That night while I slept the subway did not run at all.

***

Babysitters and bedtime stories

Before backing the next day I called Alan and asked if he could drop by and bring some cigarettes. He said that a friend of his just got mugged, and his "junkie street paranoia" had just set in, but he would ring me up on Sunday.

On Sunday morning I was awakened by the largest carillon in the world up in the sky at Riverside Church.[*] Then along came Victor and Rose — he a Ph.D. chemist, she a burgundy-haired R.N. — who brought cigarettes and took me to breakfast, down a glittering sub-freezing Broadway to 112th Street to Tom's Restaurant, well worth the hike. Keeping pace in parallel all along the way, again those cars with the deep dark tinted windows.

As we settled into a booth, I heard "Hey Wizard!" and turned to see Bob Fuhrman, COLUMBIAN yearbook editor-in-chief, formerly officially titled "The Kid," pull a scarf over his head. "You on the lam from your draft board?" Hah. Incognito without my glasses.

I happened to notice that above us the knickknack shelves on Tom's walls, usually stocked with plastic plants, now had a number of figurines of gazelles…or goats…or, no…antelopes.

…Zebras are reactionary, antelopes are missionaries…

And the zookeeper is very fond of rum.

— Simon and Garfunkel, "At the Zoo"

Later, Victor offered an observation: "The Universe is losing entropy and it seems to be ending up in your apartment."

"Your place is real cosmic too. Hey, can you tell me anything? What's happening here? Any clues? Any hints?"

"Wizard, ever read the words on the phone dial? ABC, DEF… Always Be Careful. Don't Ever Fail…."

"Jeez, thanks. That's a lotta help."

***

I needed a nap, which meant that I might get a learning experience as a bonus. Hypnopaedia happened frequently, which I came to realize via awakening, hearing voiceovers from next door through the

---

[*] Open to the public — a vertiginous climb up through the tower on open iron stairs. I recall pausing in the ascent next to the Laura Spelman Rockefeller memorial bell, size of a small cast bronze room, walls as thick as my trunk, when it sounded the quarter hour and imparted an overpowering visceral sensation of A#.

bedroom wall or up in the living room Morris chair. Interpretation was obvious. Imagery was intense. Symbolism was clear and simple. Dream along with me:

➤ Columbus or some other circle, surrounded by flatbed tractor trailers driven by cowboys in sunglasses, hauling the mammoth yachts that come in to town once a year for the Boat Show, the trucks driving faster and the circle drawing tighter as I duck and dodge until I am about to be keelhauled and then....

➤ Riding low over the city atop a gargantuan aircraft, surrounded and stunned by brilliant lights and vivid visions, then telling the pilot which way to turn. "Don't argue with the Pilot. If you cause a problem, they chop your head off and you ride the buses." Sudden fall into a bizarre hobo jungle with headless spotted horses prancing around and a railroad bull flashing his badge, and then....

➤ Massive shadowed man carrying a body bag down stairs. Intercut a *Daily News* headline: "**VALACHI, MOB'S CANARY, DIES**." Push in on man and body bag; Vinnie's voiceover: "When the cops have an important carry, they call a guy named 'Shoulder.' He's the official unofficial helper for the big assist-on-carry jobs. Shoulder cares about the dead the way regular people care about the living...." Push in on plain benign face, pan to burden on his back....

➤ Boxes, bins, conveyor belts of mail all around me; curious, I take a peek. Title punching out *à la* Teletype:

"D o n 't R e a d L e t t e r s."

Obviously not. Read words, read phrases, read sentences. After all, this *is* sorta Sesame Street.

➤ Cattle country, herds to the horizon, voiceover says that among Jim Ling The Cowboy's holdings is the King Ranch, bigger than some small states. Therefore, another principle: "Keep It Kosher," which I think meant ethics more than diet. "However," the voiceover added, "This applies only if they, uh, Hold You Up."

➤ On another Western set, with shooting coming from all sides; I am standing out in the middle of every field of fire. Conflict resolution: "Gunfight? OK. Corral." Even the letters **"OK"** form a pictogram.

➤ The Son Tay POW camp rescue attempt. On my office bulletin board I had tacked the *Times* front page photo of crewcut Col. Arthur "Bull" Simons, "the Army's leading exponent of derring-do," and the story — lead chopper deliberately crash-landed in the camp, breaking one trooper's leg; attack, search, failure: the prisoners had been moved. In this version, the location was Leslie Park back home: I was descending from the sky, raking the lawn with submachinegun fire, and then....

This last apparition got me stood up straight out of the Morris chair and backing again.

***

By now I had started singing while upping and backing, to help pass the time, distract the mind, goose the motivation, and maybe not least to impress or amuse my unseen taskmasters. From random numbers I went to entire musical comedy scores...then folk and pop tunes in alphabetical order...then medleys by composer or artist...running through my whole encyclopedic eclectic repertoire with few if any repeats.

Leslee and Donna came by of an evening, bringing packs of Tiparillos I had asked for (original, aromatic, and syrupy cherry flavors) to use as cigarette methadone. I had since exhausted the obsessive search — in rubbish, behind radiators, inside-out pockets — for any stale forgotten leftover cig or discarded butt. Cigars had been recommended some time ago as nicotine maintenance and oral/manual/tracheal pacifiers by a heavy-smoking, tapering American Tobacco writer.

I had to ask them: "What day is today?" I really didn't know. They took me down to the Gold Rail*, trusty old campus saloon, for a

---

* One campus then supported only two sizeable bars. The Gold Rail, as wood-panel-generic as saloons get, with a better-than-average menu, reasonable prices, and friendly service, was frequented by jocks and serious drinkers. The West End, where Ginsberg, Kerouac, *et al.* hung out, attracted a classier clientele, plus those unwilling to walk four blocks down to the Rail. Other, smaller gin mills catered to the indigenous black and white working class; much Hispanic community drinking involved paper-bagged beers consumed on corners.

burger, but this meant walking down Broadway, so I had us cut across before we passed Riverside Church, lest it fall on me, then back across again, explaining that I was superstitious.

"Now listen to this!" from somewhere in the background as we sat down in a booth at the Gold Rail.

"Ya gotta understand, I'm doing the best I can," I said to Leslee and Donna over the first mild beer. "I'm really trying. Uh, was I OK on the way down?"

"It hardly matters," Donna said, her edged voice honed and stropped even sharper than usual. "It hardly matters."

"I don't know what's happening here but I'm doing the best I can. Honest to God. Somebody oughta let somebody know that."

"What day is today?" I heard from a booth nearby.

I thanked Donna and Leslee for the burger and the two beers, although obtaining the second one took a little wheedling. "Sing for your supper and you'll get breakfast," I quoted from *The Boys From Syracuse.* Oops. The line all but shouted the Agency's initials. SSCandB. Too close for comfort.

Back at 45 Tiemann Place, on the table in the lobby there was a blow-in TIME-LIFE subscription card with a bold thumbprint on the mailing face. Aww, shit.

The next morning for breakfast I cracked open a fresh pack of Tiparillos and lit one up. In fifteen minutes my stomach bulged with gas, my mouth twinged with nausea. I had to barf. No I didn't. Just a good belch. That just made it worse. It'll go away. But when? I'll get over it. Maybe, maybe not. Urp. Really not that bad. Ohhh. Yes it is. I can keep it down. But do I want to? I gotta barf.

I knelt at the toilet and threw up at will. The vomitus was scant. The action was effortless and painless. The impression and association were unforgettable and inseparable: smoke, then barf.

OK. Got it. I recognized aversion therapy: cigar spiked with a strong, harmless emetic. But whom did I have to thank? Leslee, psychology grad student that she was? Nahh. Too conscientious, too kindly. Donna? Unlikely: she was an occasional smoker. The *bodega* that sold the cigars? *No sabe.* The Agency? Who knows?

Whoever, I appreciate it. Dubiously ethical but definitely downright goddam effective. After a week of averse abstention the breath came clear, cold, deep and delicious. I suddenly said out loud, "Hey! How 'bout that! I don't smoke! *I don't smoke!*"[*]

* * *

---

[*] Another coincidence: Mike the Mailman gave me a lift to the airport after Christmas, and his wife fixed me a cold turkey sandwich to nosh along the way.

Appointed rounds and 'round and 'round

Both Bill Timm and Don Booth called and asked me to see the company doctor. After some fencing with them I called the doc, hearing her say to a departing patient, "Just bring your head, honey," one of Leslee's shrink's trademark expressions. I made an appointment for that evening, and Leslee invited me to come over afterward to visit her and her *simpatica* roommates at 380 Riverside Drive, one of my favorite refuges.

Getting ready, I slipped on a puddle of spilled water or coffee. Up from the airshaft came the comment, "At least he knows he can't walk on water." Without my glasses, I kept getting hung up on various things, and started to lose track of the time. Then a knock at the door: uniformed cop says he's looking for a burglar.

"Nobody by that description here, officer."

"You know you have a hole in your bathroom window: they could get in through there."

"They wouldn't get any further: I put a padlock on the bathroom. They're welcome to anything they can find there."

"Yeah. Hey, this must be yours."

The new phone directory had just been delivered outside the door. He handed it to me — Peter Maxish cover art and the headline

Do It By The Book.

Finally I ducked into the closet, popped out all suited up, and set out, headed for the Broadway bus. There it was down the street sitting right at the corner, but then a neon sign in the Hispanic beauty shop window blinked and the bus pulled away. So I took the train and transferred toward unfamiliar territory, the upper East Side, where a fella on the subway gestured with his newspaper: "Follow your nose." No glasses, no landmarks, no help: somehow I ended up on back on the wrong side of town on Central Park West.

I started to cross the park on foot[*], but was warded off by a woman walking her dog and hollering "No!" in a voice that sounded like Swazey's. Finally a crosstown bus came along and I got on, without exact change, and was carried through the park.

The doctor was not in, I was informed by the white-coated, glaring-glassed guy who answered the office door. Oddly, he resembled one Dewey Deavers, professional hypnotist and lifeguard at the Boys' Club pool back home.

A long walk through the brittle cold night into Midtown, into another guided tour, but this time led around by more than a fleet of cars and trucks. I discovered that the Cowboy's cabs were people too. At Third Avenue in the 50s, near the new FDR Station P.O., a voice in the Euro-Israeli accent of Bella the Landlord: "He must be looking for his Pist Office."

Headed up an avenue that I evidently should have been going down: "How's THAT for knowing your own mind?" Aloud, I blurted "Manley W. Nelson!" Manley had been an account executive on Lysol, previously a colleague of Ron Ziegler at J. Walter Thompson in L.A., which is where I thought he had gone back to. What's *he* doing here?

In the Channel Gardens at Rockefeller Center, sounding like my cousin Georgie from Jersey, "Exceptionally well!" On a side street westward to Times Square, "I went to San Francisco but I...*left* real soon." OK. Hard left, back around.

Around a corner, a beat cop was saying to some kids, "Keep it moving, Johnny." Keep it moving. I kept marching through the Midtown night with shoulders shivering, feet numbing, then burning. Any block now I expected someone to come by, pick me up, and carry me to 380 Riverside, which is where the party must be. Or at

---

[*] Not as bold or foolhardy as it might sound. On summer nights I occasionally traipsed through the Park, albeit in the company of a few other guys, none especially imposing, all of us at least a little under the influence of one or another chemical. By far the most memorable expedition: Sheep Meadow, the night before the Apollo 11 moon landing, as the networks set up their triangle of plank projection screens. NBC tested the picture with its on-the-air Saturday Night at the Movies, "North to Alaska," starring John Wayne. Imagine a drive-in — walk-in — theater right in the middle of a July Manhattan night.

least I awaited some sign that this particular exercise or demonstration or lesson or test was completed.

For a while I shrank under the pyramidal overhang of a nearly finished building, 110 W. 42$\underline{^{nd}}$ off Fifth, then into the partial shelter of a corner of a loading dock, then into a dark doorway. Two men walked past: "When we're done, let's go up to the *joint*." The joint, huh? OK. Back to West 42$\underline{^{nd}}$, seeking the light of the Crossroads of the World. Two women walked past: "*Dobranoc.*"

"*Dobranoc.*"

"*Dobranoc!*" *"Good night"* in Polish!

I dropped down into the next subway entrance I saw, into a little shopping arcade, the token booth and turnstiles well down the hall. The shops all had green ecology flag decals on the doors. One had a photocopy of a commemorative stamp, "American Wool, U.S. Postage, 13¢," dated January 22. For whatever it meant, I recalled that Don Booth had asked me to keep January 22 open for a radio seminar.

The subway was within sight, but for want of a 40¢ fare, beyond reach. I had spent all my tokens and change in getting downtown and crosstown and lost, also passing out the odd leftover nickels and dimes to a friendly swarm of little kid panhandlers. Jumping a turnstile or entering through an exit gate was a risk, last resort, and most important, cheating on the test.

Then I realized that I was wearing my herringbone Chesterfield topcoat. (The velvet collar, originally a symbol of mourning, also known as "The Yoke," after the Scripture, "My yoke is sweet and my burden is light" — implicit, "Take Care of the Big Secret." Unbeknownst to me when I bought it[*], the Chesterfield turned out to be something of a uniform for those people striding around Midtown.)

The coat had a little hole in the change pocket, and consequently, some coins trickled through and stuck all the way down in the corner, hard enough to get at that they had not been worth the trouble of retrieving before. But now, with fishing and fretting and a little ripping apart the lining, after about ten minutes I came up with a

---

[*] October, 1969, $88.00 at Halstan Ltd., on Broadway across from campus — not to be confused with the designer, unless owner flashes label quickly but conspicuously. The salesman mentioned that I could have the collar removed at any time.

couple of tokens and quarters and was soon on the platform waiting for the train.

American wool.

Two naval officers walked along the platform, talking earnestly:

"You need to have an equalizer."

"He's *got* an equalizer."

In front of the apartment building was a van marked "Port Electric." I turned on the radio to a clever little show that kept me company most of the night.

***

Don't look back

"Any way you look at it, you lose." The backing always, always finished with failure. That was the point. That was how negative motivation worked. No win, no way.

The catch came from the story of the plot to kidnap Henry Kissinger, specifically the collection of items found in the suspect's quarters: images of Franklin D. Roosevelt, pens and pencils, glass-cutting instruments. After every exercise, one of these would turn up on the bathroom floor and the heart would plummet into the stomach. I tried to prevent that by gathering and stashing all the razor blades, knives, scissors and such on the premises. (All the pens in the house seemed to have disappeared.) At the end of the next round they planted a neatly cut oblong of sheet glass. After another, they just tossed a dime in through the hole in the bathroom window. Image of FDR indeed.

I forget what I did wrong in one sequence, but the response was memorable. Suddenly there was rapid-fire hammering right at the bottom of my door. I felt and saw the nails as yellow flashes driving into the top of my head, which hurt from my scalp to my eyeballs. A voice outside: "See how you like getting trapped in one of these." (Oh. Like a mailbox.) To this day I really hate hammering noises.

Out of orneriness one afternoon I reversed the process — went up on my back, down on my belly. At that, from up atop the 125th Street subway platform, the air raid siren sounded. The siren blew frequently — as often as I did something contrary. Tumbling, for example — for variety and showbiz nostalgia, since my mother almost married into the Hamid Family, and I could have been a circus acrobat. Tumbling was discouraged.

For one set, I had to move in time with the sound of a basketball bouncing down in the courtyard and thumping up the airshaft. "This is stupid," I muttered when I couldn't keep up, so I sat down. "You know I'm not a jock." The siren cried. In another instance I got cranky about noises outside, and hollered in my bombasso command voice, "I can make more noise than you can!" Oh yeah? In seconds an airliner just leaving LaGuardia departure control dropped down low and buzzed the building, slamming the apartment and me with a 100 dBA cannonade.

Ultimately I stood up on my hind legs. "I'm not crawling any more." And I didn't. I got to walk. But soon this got boring, just mechanistic pacing. About the best I could do to make a statement was to shuffle and trace an upside-down omega thus Ω — symbolically citing Ohm's Law along the pattern of the hooked rug in the bedroom. Then Leslee called and asked what I was doing. "I am *resisting*."

"Have you thought of doing any typing?"

"Uhhh...." Aha. Semicircle sidestep for the keys, slide straight across for the carriage return.

Eventually I took to saying the rosary as I kept pace. One night, all night, the cues had me scampering back and forth in the dark[*] until a little light came through the windows and I could go to bed. Another gloom of night, the apartment filled with fog, visibility less than one foot.

For some special occasion, the airshaft spewed out horrific bestial and human sounds, bizarre music, stalking shadows and *scherzo* lights. On that St. Walpurgisnacht, I half expected someone or something to come in through the window. I was ready for that. Come on. Come and get it. Whoever came in would have met a top-of-the-lungs bellow, loud enough to blow them off the fire escape.

Later the training presented a novel test: outside the door, someone said "It may not be long." Ahh. A timed test. An endurance test. But every time I decided enough was enough and stopped, they reset their clock. From that I discovered that when one paces for hours nonstop from the bathroom to the bedroom's French doors and back and forth, the body begins to feel virtually weightless, almost free-falling up and down, just visual zooming with little or no sensation of using the feet and legs until finally they turned to rubber and went out from under me. The very second I folded to the floor, the steam came up in the pipes.

All the backing, opening, and closing shined up the bathroom doorknob from verdigris to burnished bronze, and shook loose the

---

[*] I could actually get around well in the dark: in fact, I could get fully dressed in total darkness, finding and coordinating clothes by feel. This came from a summer's experience as a counselor at a blind kids' camp, where light was a frill for the sighted. The kids could read in the dark, with a rustle of Braille pages turning under covers after taps. At least I hoped the kids were turning pages.

little lathed piece of wood that kept the bathroom door from banging against the tile wall. I seized upon that and wielded it like a relay baton up and down, backing or bellying or standing. Swazey asked "What is that — a doll that you're carrying around?" "No, Mizz Swazey. It's a doorstop." Up yours, Donald Edward John Wilkes Booth.

Racket in the hall: beating on the door, shouting, then prying, nails creaking, wood splitting. Panic: they're coming in -- what do I do? The thin safety panel came out of the door and in bounded four or five or six cops. "Is there a burglar in here? We're looking for a burglar. Who are you? What are you doing here?"

"I live here."

"You call this living? You got any I.D.?"

"Lost my wallet somewhere." (Originally I did have it tucked in the bookcase, but then it was gone. Hard to get anywhere without cash and I.D.) "Look, officer: there's my picture on the wall." 30" x 40" blowup, birthday present from Kirk, Jan, and Leslee, grinning portrait in sweatshirt with beer, which I headed in Helvetica Bold Prestype®,

El Wizard
para Alcalde
(The Wizard for Mayor.)

"*El Wizard*? Hey...*Wizzid*...you got anything with your *real* name on it?"

"Errrr....OK, here's my checkbook." The cop snatched it.

"Where's the bank?"

"750 Third Avenue, right around the corner from the 1-7. Fine precinct."

Then in came Bella the Landlord and Mr. Miller the Super, who verified that I did in fact live there. But the cops had to follow through somehow. A young bulked-up officer said, "Whassamatta with you, huh? You, *Wizzid*. Normal people don't live like this. You're living like a cave man a million years ago. You better have this place cleaned up by tomorrow because I'm sending the Board of Health up here, and the Fire Department, and the Sanitation Department, and the building inspector. *Wizzid.*"

(Officer, I have been crawling around this place in the dark and I can barely see the garbage, much less the dirt, let alone clean anything

104

up or throw anything away. Nor have I had the chance to shave or comb my hair or coordinate my outfit. If I knew you were coming…. Incidentally, if you were looking for a real burglar, you'd have come in here with pistols drawn or at least sticks out, and you would have considered and treated me as dangerous until proven otherwise.[*])

Then it was Bella's turn. "Vishnyevskee" — she was one of the few people outside the old neighborhood to pronounce the name in proper pickled-tongue Polish — "You are not the handsome young man I remember in this apartment. What is wrong with you? Do you use dopes?"

I looked plaintively at Mr. Miller. Sheesh. Everybody uses dopes. "Naw, Bella, he doesn't use dopes."

<<WHEW>>

"Vishnyevskee, you do not look good. *Jak si masz?* How are you? Are you sick?," Bella asked. "You should see a doctor."

"Yes, Mrs. Geliebter. I plan to. Thank you for your concern."

They had a lease they wanted me to sign (rent increased $3 to $111.91/mo. for "reviring, repiping, and maintenance the building") and I said I would be happy to, and make out a check for the rent, but I couldn't seem to find a pen (no pens, no messages to the outside), so I borrowed one of theirs. As they left, I noticed that both were wearing black overcoats and black hats.

Who's that yonder dressed in black?
Must be the hypocrites turning back.
Go tell it on the mountain, to let my people go!

<<How does the song go? "Go Where I Send Thee," "Green Grow The Rushes," "Who Singeth Thirteen?">>

Alex the Porter came in. "Hey Polack!" <<POLACK?>> He gave me one of his burlap squares to gather the garbage, adding "I'll come by and he'p you." Hey, I need all the he'p I can get. I'm living like a cave man from a million years ago.

---

[*] By the way, officer, I didn't give myself the name "Wizard." That got hung on me by my tutees (Humanities, Contemporary Civilization, English A, ghosted girlfriend letters) on the freshman football team. One of them ultimately led the nation in total offense his senior year (Columbia had no other offense to speak of), became an NFL first-round draft pick, thanked me in public for making his career possible, and backed up Johnny Unitas. So there.

Old Mark and Leslee seemed to share that impression when they visited one night. I was glutting up a big pot of beans, soaked and baked from scratch from Jan and Kirk's leavebehinds, which I welcomed as survival rations, ultimately going through the tuna fish, rice, and noodles, and the figs having gone through me.

"We'll take you to dinner. Anywhere you wanna go."

"Naw. This is fine. Want some?"

"How can you eat that shit, Wizard?"

"This is like communion."

Old Mark had brought along a letter that my brother had for whatever reason addressed to me at the shop. I noted the postmark and mounted my high horse.

"How long has this been down there?"

"Maybe a week."

"How come you didn't forward it? See that return address? That's my *brother*. You know about him. My brother the junkie. See that number next to his name — and 'Box 2000, Lexington, Kentucky 40507'? That's a federal hospital. See that stamp? That's an American flag. This was conveyed to you by an agency of the United States Government, and you are legally bound to ensure that it reaches the person to whom it is addressed. You knew where I was. Jeez."

When they left I read the letter, looking for something between the lines. A little before this adventure started, the Old Man had taken to signing his off with "Take care."

My brother, who wrote rarely, saying little, wrote here, *sic*:

Dear Jim:

I have been hearing somewhat of what happening with you and I don't believe its you that's why I'm writing the letter so in your return you can tell me whats up. Daddy is really worried about you lousing your job but fuck the job I'm worried about you. The job you have is a nice set up but if it isn't really what you want to be doing give it up and get something else you have a good enough head to do what you what to do.

I guess you want to know whats I'm doing well let me start out to say that I have myself fairly straightened up and I'm in a program and really doing good I'm really happy for once and everything is going ok if I wasn't here I would have been in New York as soon as I heard about you.

Jim you never wanted to give me sermons and I'm to young to give you one I just want to let you know and I want to know for myself that what whatever you do you have given thought and its what you want to do so before you do anything think and it will come out ok.

Jim we all really love you and anything that happens to you happens to us too. People like me and you have to stick together in life....

He signed off with "Take care.")

Old Mark said it looked like I was losing weight. He told my father it seemed like 20 or 30 pounds, which was a lot from the usual 140 or 150. Later I noticed myself that the cheekbones were getting sharp and the eyes were getting deep, so in front of the mirror I quoted the Beatles:

Blackbird singin' in the dead of night,
Take these sunken eyes and learn to see.

Then Mark mentioned that Bill Timm — "Chairman Moo" to us — had wanted me to see the company doctor. "I had an appointment but I got hung up in traffic." Then he asked how long I thought I could keep doing this. "With what I have in my savings account, I could hold out here for a year or more."

After they left, I looked out the peephole. Atop a rubbish bag in the hall I saw a loaf of bread, big "THIN" on the label. You're slicing your bread pretty thin, man. Shortly after, it occurred to me to retrieve the bread but it was gone. Point taken.

All these people dropping by unannounced. Jan stopped in and took me to dinner at the Indian restaurant just a little down Broadway. A few doors up a Spanish kid was hollering "Jimmy! Jimmy!" over and over to a window above. Another kid: "I'm depending on yoooooou."

"Doesn't this remind you of a camp?" Jan asked.

"High or low camp?" He didn't get it. I was not about to say "Oswiecim."

The restaurant was almost empty except for a few out-of-place soft-focus semi-familiar faces, and two Indian men conspicuously, affectedly smoking. Even I was most surprised that this evoked no craving, elicited no interest. Fine. I'll show 'em even more. I ordered egg curry: everyone knew I hated eggs. The only *faux pas* I committed was spooning up an entire egg and almost sucking it in whole.

At the end of the evening as Jan was leaving I had to ask: "What brings you by here, anyway?"

"I am the Seven Deadly Sins." He grinned kindly.

Mizz Swazey came by most every day, usually with a beer, on occasion with a little food ("UNEEDA" cracker), often with a proverb ("It's a great life if you don't weaken") or feedback or directions or information by association. She was sharing a bag of pretzels, Drake's, not a common brand in the market; she took a pretzel and with great flourish pointed it down at her lap.

"MAN DRAKE ROOT." Aha. Aha. Aha. Cracked your goddam code, Judy — and I wrote the goddam cypher pad. (This and other puzzles were set up in phone conversations, random remarks, graffiti, radio copy, a couple of my writing samples from school, and Swazeyisms all too involved and obscure to recount. But in this case: at the shop last summer, minor renovation was blocked off by wraparound sheets of brown paper, soon labeled "SSCandB Graffiti Wall." For a creative department, the entries were disappointing ("Down with BBDO!", "Why is this brown?", "Dick Uhl is a *good* writer!"), so I had to add lines like "Free the Indianapolis 500!", "Ted Gold died for your sins," and Donne:

> *Go and catch a falling star,*
> *Get with child a mandrake root,*
> *Tell me where all past years are,*
> *Or who cleft the devil's foot...*
> *If thou beest born to strange sights*
> *Things invisible to see*
> *Ride ten thousand days and nights*
> *Till age snow white hairs on thee,*
> *Thou, when thou return'st, wilt tell me*
> *All strange wonders that befell thee*
> *And swear*
> *No where*
> *Lives a woman true and fair....*

and so forth, in full, leading one of the overdone fashion writers to remark as she recognized it, "Someone must be having girlfriend problems."

✻✻✻

Mizz Swazey would often sing a line or two. In some context she alluded to Dr. Strangelove, and crooned "I wonder who's…"

"I wonder who's Kissinger now."

✻✻✻

Judy Appleton called shortly thereafter and told me, "You have good marks." So I did: from the backing, a widow's-peak-style scab about two inches long on the forehead, and a gash gouged into the outside edge of the right hand. Good marks. Plus she and I knew I had always had good grades.

✻✻✻

Riding the underground railroad

A New York City Transit Authority subway token, solid brass, is marked "Good For One Fare," which can be good for upwards of six hundred miles in transit. I loved the trains — the mass, the metal, the momentum, four thousand horsepower, three to four hundred tons, air brakes releasing, then the long machine accelerating 0 to 40 mph in 30 seconds, from switching to series to multiple speeds, projecting along the constant unchangeable course of the tunnels, the turning of the great coiled motors and forged iron traction caught and compressed to an impenetrable density of sound and enveloping amplitude of vibration, with bare bulb lights and plain color signals pointing periodic moments of passage for a mile or two to another sudden lit-up room along the way.

I wondered at the endless Mobius procession of people coming and going, a thousand or more a trainful, people I had never seen before and would never see again, all new and nameless, all sorts, different types at different stops at given times, people waiting and boarding and departing into their unknown, unknowable lives in the unseen imagined places up above the ground. All these people, all this pluralism on one path: together we go where the train goes.

I respected the system, from the scale and scope and public works weight of the civil engineering, to details like the decorative Dutchy faience and the ornamental wrought ironwork, to the relentless, ceaseless operation, around the clock, all around, under and over the town. Norman Mailer and Jimmy Breslin running for Mayor envisioned an urban monorail. Who were they kidding? We had one on three rails. It was a privilege to ride these trains, I thought, and it could be an adventure.

***

You could do pretty much whatever you wanted in the subways, except

> ## PLEASE KEEP HANDS || OFF THE DOORS

```
┌─────────────────────────────────────────────┐
│                                               │
│         PASSENGERS ARE FORBIDDEN              │
│         TO RIDE BETWEEN CARS                  │
│                                               │
└─────────────────────────────────────────────┘
```

Staying off the right-of-way went without saying. Also,

```
┌─────────────────────────┐
│                         │
│      NO SMOKING         │
│      NO SPITTING        │
│                         │
└─────────────────────────┘
```

though I did see cops and motormen lighting up openly at the ends of their lines. Otherwise, eating, drinking, sleeping, singing, dancing — almost anything goes.

The trains became part of the trial and the testing. My expeditions into the underworld:

▮▶   The mission: go as far as you can and back on one token, so Mizz Swazey seems to say in so many words. Four boroughs (Staten Island would have been a side trip), 10¢ a borough. Feasible enough in theory, but with no map, not much vision, and the entire IND and BMT lines *terra incognita,* not to mention all of Brooklyn except Bay Ridge, and all of Queens except the way to Shea Stadium, *not* easy. For guidance I do remember the lyric of "Subway Directions" from *Subways Are For Sleeping:*

Uptown by local to Van Cortlandt Parkway,

Get up, cross over, go down....

Good enough a start as any. Or should it be downtown to Flatbush or New Lots in Brooklyn...or crosstown and under to Queens through Jamaica...or....? This takes several midcourse corrections to get right, not just plotting the transfers and making the connections, but moving with a sense of purpose and, absolutely essentially, perseverance.

The trains can be hard on the ears, the seat, the spirit. Indeterminate hours can be worse. It is easy enough to bail out, get up, cross over, go down, go home. Who really needs to go to the outer limits of the outer boroughs anyhow? I mean, really — what's the

111

point? If I can get to Gun Hill Road, that's quite far enough toward the end of the Bronx. Evidently not quite. The objective was to go all the way.

The trips are not travelogue material. A tunnel is a tunnel. Seen one station, seen hundreds. The fine distinctions between ACF (American Car & Foundry) and St. Louis Car Co. cars, the unique brand identities of IRT, IND, BMT lines, the finesse of motormen with their handles or the timbre of conductors in their announcements: those are for buffs at leisure. Even at and above grade, the trains at night do not show much of the city, nor its best sides.

But we are all tourists in this Capital of Civilization, and some sights are always remarkable. The A Train: stainless steel full speed flat out nonstop straight from 125th Street and St. Nicholas Avenue to 59th Street and Columbus Circle or vice versa, deserving the theme song. Deep beneath lower Manhattan, the enormous domed cavern of Chambers Street. The archaeology of ghost stations, closed, sealed, preserved as catacombs. The labyrinthine junctions — Times Square, Grand Central — steel lines and strung lights every which way. Right upon surfacing in the Bronx, Yankee Stadium hoving up huge and white. Spread across the outskirts, the vast transit yards, acres of iron rows with all the system's rolling stock lined up at rest and ready. Far Rockaway, where the city becomes an oceanside village on creosoted piers in tidal marsh. The glorious cityscape seen from the wondrous working monument of the Great Bridge. The very railroad itself, the continuing constant, millions in perpetual motion. All-expense-paid round trip 40¢, no reservations necessary.

▐▶ Guidance from graffiti and advertising posters along the itinerary. If I get off where I shouldn't, or try to transfer where I can't, I see a 1-sheet media ad headed

HN1050. You Got The Wrong Station,
or
HN1050. Stick It In Your Ear.
On the right track, headway:
HN1050. For Traffic Headaches.
HN1050. We're With You.
HN1050. Starts In Any Weather.
Brass starts in any weather. The brass token. The electric brass.

112

To show me where to get off, flyer for a rock group:

THE ELEPHANT'S MEMORY
TAKES TO THE STREETS.

▐▶ At the outset of one of these forays, up on the 125th Street platform, I have an umbrella with me. Aha. I pound the tip against the planks once, twice. Hey, why not? Saw it work once. By God it works again. A downtown train pulls right out of the tunnel.

▐▶ End of the line in the Bronx, middle of the graveyard shift, waiting for the next southbound local, I hear a conductor call out, "Regular coffee, four sugars for Motorman Young." That was the same coffee I ordered every morning at Chock Full o' Nuts. Motorman Young. O my. Simon and Garfunkel:
They call me "Baby Driver," and once upon a pair of wheels....

▐▶ Late night, Broadway/7th Avenue Express, TA cop finds a passenger asleep, taps his foot with his nightstick, and says "Get outta the monkey house! Go and ride the local!" Purgatory.

▐▶ The easy way to Queens is the No. 7 straight from Grand Central to the World's Fair grounds and Shea Stadium. Too easy. I am waiting for the train when two guys come downstairs asking loudly, "Where do you EAT?" Oh. It's the *Flushing* line. OK. I'll go another way. This is pointed out by a fella walking by, wearing a field jacket with a division patch: sword topped by the legend "FOLLOW ME." In transit: a Russian-language newspaper, the popular Hoboe Coboe, strewn over the car floor, with a grey-wooled West Point cadet seated nearby, so in symbolic demonstration I stomp and grind my heel on the Cyrillic.

▐▶ Deserted station, formidable black figure looms down the platform and calls out to me, "Hey! Mister President!" Great. All I need here now is a drunk or a nut or a panhandler. He rolls right up to me and in a soft civil voice says, "Hey, President Lincoln. You're

OK. Take care, man," and claps me on the shoulders. Yeah. Gaunt face, short beard, dark coat, tall: there is a resemblance.[*]

▥▶ Early morning somewhere out in Queens aboard a very old train — hump-backed red brown body, wooden and wicker seats — but even at high speed, motors no more than murmuring, running straight, true, and slick, like an antique car on a factory-special new chassis. Unusual load of riders for this hour: too fresh, too polite, too upscale, with a formalized way of coming aboard, taking a strap, taking a seat. I start to think that Ling puts the best rolling stock in service when his people go to work. I'll take a Chance (Vought).

▥▶ Old man starts a sob story on a train and continues it following me off to the express platform. Jimmy Foy, he says he is. "I remember the Seven Little Foys," I allow. Then his pants fall down.

"Hey, pal, lemme help ya. I got a spare belt here," which I did, but it doesn't fit Jimmy Foy. His topcoat label reads "Rogers Peet": at least this is a better class of lost soul. His right leg looks like a pink paper mailing tube.

Nobody has troubles like Jimmy Foy. He wanted to be a doctor but got polio. Tonight he says he has been rolled by a prostitute, claims he is sick and wants to go to a hospital. I suggest that he wants to go home and go to bed. Then a TA cop, decorations stacked above his shield, comes on the scene. "This a friend of yours?"

"Met him on the subway."

"Oh. That kinda friend."

"Yeah. He's, uh, not feeling too good, y'know, like that."

Jimmy asks the cop to take him to a hospital. Cop says he shouldn't take up a hospital bed that a really sick person really needs. Jimmy casts aspersions on the cop's intelligence or youth or something. Cop tenses.

---

[*] Which I have exploited on many Hallowe'ens since, needing only a stovepipe, grosgrain tie, fringed wool shawl atop an old dark suit and wornout white shirt, sometimes a cane and a volume of Sandburg tucked under the arm for effect. In a restaurant, hostess summoned dishwashers out of the kitchen, pointed to me and said "See? He freed you a hundred years ago and you haven't done a lick of work since!" They cracked up.

"Jeez, Jimmy. Show a little respect for the badge. He's just doin' his job here. Jeez. Officer, he's OK — just a little, uh, y'know...."

"I'm sick. I wanna go to the hospital."

"Jeez, Jimmy. You just need to go to bed."

Jimmy gets to choose between sleeping it off at home or in the Transit Authority lockup, which would waste the cop's time and ruin Jimmy's day or week once he realized what day or year it was. Since Jimmy is in no shape to make a sound decision, I volunteer. "I'll get him home, officer. You got better things to do."

Home is Vermilyea Avenue in the Bronx. ("Vermilion Avenoo?" "*Vermilyea* Avenoo. Ver-**MIL**-yah. V...e...r...m...i...l...y...e...a. Vermilyea.") I know how to get to the Bronx, but that's it; between unscrambling Jimmy's directions and outsmarting myself, I get us on the wrong train going in the wrong direction.

The sky is getting light as we two-step down the stairs from the elevated platform in the Bronx, Jimmy holding up his pants with one hand, his other arm over my shoulder holding himself up. I have gotten us off one stop too far, so we get a good healthy morning walk. Midway is a diner where I buy us some coffee, whereupon Jimmy decides he should take his medicine, spilling a mittful of pills, three or four colors worth, over the counter and onto the floor. I suggest that maybe he should wait a while and make sure he's taking what he needs to take.

Vermilyea Avenue. Never heard of it before. Nice clean modest Bronx block. He wants me to come in, visit for a while, meet Mrs. Foy, have some breakfast, she always has coffee on. I tell him thanks, and it would be a pleasure, and I'd love to, but I oughta be getting home, maybe next time I see ya.

We get to the door of his apartment, I shake his hand and he's home. From down the dark hallway a lady says, "Thanks, Mister."

➤ March 8, 1971, the COLUMBIAN yearbook office, hanging out. In the Garden, the first Ali-Frazier fight has just been decided. After reporting the results, the radio plays a timely Simon and Garfunkel selection, "The Boxer":

...."I am leaving, I am leaving,"
But the fighter still remains.

("I am leaving": Leslee's phrase for paging through a book. "...still remains" ... "remains still," similar syntax to "I understand"..."I stand under" [the Big T.])

Then the station jingle ID: **"HN-1050! Hear it!"** Even here. Even on their radio here.

No surprise in the song, not at all. Shouldn't wonder. Always thought of the lyric as an ashcan school capsule (5:07) bio, now more than ever.

The radio describes the crowd in the Garden chanting "Joe! Joe!" "Ahhh---leee! Ahhh---leee!" Then the song chorus, and again, "HN-1050! Hear it!"

Later Mr. Henry the Janitor comes in and we b.s. a little, as we have done many late nights here. There is something he suggests about Frazier answering the bell with a broken jaw, or Ali fighting with a broken hand, and some *shtick* on the radio, that seems to send me to the Bronx.

I am either on the A or the D train, 'way uptown, sitting in the corner of a standing-room-only car. Not hard to notice that I am the only whitey, a 1% minority here, and everyone else looks like they have a problem with my ofay presence. So I set my face, focus off into the middle distance, and start chanting to myself, "Joe! Joe! Ahhh-leee! Ahhh-leee!" This works just fine. Linebacker in a leather coat takes a position alongside me — these companions seem to show up a lot — and the inner chant swells. I am not afraid of anything anymore. I cannot come to harm.

 From the East River, the World Trade Center under construction, lights scattered all through the open high steel, but at the top of a tower, up and big and bright enough to see from Brooklyn and beyond, the lights form a symbol:

∞

***

West Side stories

I guessed it was a Friday or Saturday night. "A man's got a right to get out in the halls once a week," someone declared out in my hall, whereupon the phone rang and my old semi-pal Larry invited me to stop by his Carman Hall dorm room. On my way out, I heard Elton John from a nearby apartment:

And now that it's over, I hope you don't mind,

I hope you don't mind....

That could be interpreted in several ways, which of course I did, understanding that "And now that it's over" had to be a feint, and I'd better mind.

At Larry's I was given M&Ms sorted by color, Dr. Pepper, and a little stuff. I kept thinking I was giving out secrets, self-doubt dope-induced, but actually only dropped M&Ms. Later Larry and I went to see Jon Kandel, then producing the Columbia *Spectator* daily paper (aspiring *New York Times Jr.,* mostly in the "Do as the *Times* Romans do" mode). As entertainment, the two of them overdid a bafflegab non-working demo of the new punchtape computer typesetter. Here there were donuts and more Dr. Pepper, but I dropped donut shards all over, then happened to back up and sit on a can of Dr. Pepper planted directly below my butt.

"WOW!" (which is "MOM" upside down, and there goes your food), Larry admonished in a hard whisper.

"Hey, somebody *put* that there," I replied in a harder whisper.

From there we got into Larry's car and headed down to the NYU Medical School, right alongside Bellevue, to visit David Debs Bogorad, less manic as a med student than he had been as our yearbook Editor-in-Chief. All the way across town and down, Larry driving like a compulsive cowboy, the cars and lights swarmed around us. Now that it's over, I had my glasses on. I really wanted to see out. I had really been off the streets for six weeks or more. But evidently, as Larry dropped heavy and heavier hints, the glasses had to come off.

All we did in the tiny dim dorm room was sit on the floor and watch TV. Very odd. Johnny Carson was a sequence of jumpy splices, which seemed to cut and pan keyed to my movements. On another channel, guy being stalked by a giant spider* in a bad B/W horror movie. I found myself much more interested in the stack of papers next to David's rubbish — hadn't seen the *Times* in weeks — but as I ruffled through the papers, the spider closed in. Oh. I get it. Moved away from the papers, and instantly, on the TV, "He is no longer afraid of the spider monster."

On the way out, David took us through a basement to a padlocked stainless walk-in freezer door. "That's where they keep the *bodies*." His parting words: "It all depends on the amount consumed and the means of consumption." Yeah. But that was one of his standard lines anyway. I would have preferred our communal, universal standard, from *The Wild Bunch*: "It ain't like it used to be, but it'll do."

***

I attempted escapes. The first seemed to be Swazey's idea: she said I should really get away from all this and go home where I belonged, which seemed to be the best course at the time, but when I got to the subway escalator I found it blocked by a velvet rope. Stopped hard.

For the next attempt, I took my half-round trip leftover Pittsburgh-to-New York bus ticket down to the Port Authority Terminal, and asked to exchange it for a one-way to Pittsburgh, but Greyhound wanted a $5 surcharge, which I didn't have. Third try: the Pennsylvania Railroad, which refused to take my check. "No wonder you're going bankrupt," I observed to the ticket agent.

I tried to call the Old Man, not for funds, which I would not ask for in principle, but for advice, which I, even I, was ready to admit I needed, even from him. The call was disconnected as soon as it was dialed. No help.

Finally I came across my wallet (returned to the same spot in the bookcase where I had stashed it in January), and figured now I could cash a check at the nearby convenient 125th Street Chemical Bank branch. Beyond my mishmash assortment of I.D.s (Social Security card, draft card, Blue Cross/Blue Shield card, press card, Columbia Rifle Club membership card, old bank statement, canceled checks, family picture), the bank officer wanted to know if anyone knew me in the office on down on 3rd Avenue. I mentioned that someone

---

* Giant, regular, or mite-size, to this day my all-time favorite phobia

named Eisenhauer originally opened the account for me. The platform officer called for verification, although the conversation was entirely one-sided, since the button on his phone wasn't lit.

I eventually walked out with $50 of my own money, but the next day, I saw a graffito on a Chemical Bank subway poster: "Site of the Big Ripoff". Hey. As soon as I was ready to buy a ticket to ride, Bogorad called up: "Wizzie, I know this guy who got R&R, but it was only for a week and then he had to come back." A *week*. Nuts.

I tried at least to evade surveillance. On the living room window next to my Morris chair was a photocell switch gadget which the Old Man had ostensibly gotten as a premium from a dental supply house. He gave it to me to turn a light on automatically when it got dark outside, which he thought might be a real deterrent to the local burglars. I figured if nothing else it would startle and scatter the roaches that hung out under the lampshade and amid the detritus in and around the chair.

When I installed it, the nameplate ("Sens-O-Light" or similar bland brand name) snapped off, revealing another trademark — "Sentinel," a strong performance promise. But eventually I began to suspect that there was more to this gadget than met the photoelectric eye. Many things I said in the apartment, even to myself, were being played back outside. Someone outside seemed to know where I was in the flat, even in the dark, in motion, on my belly or tiptoeing in my stocking feet. And as I napped in the chair, I had had that vivid vignetted dream about the Son Tay rescue staged in the hometown park; as I woke up, I thought I was still hearing automatic weapons fire.

Oho. This little box, half the size of a pack of smokes, must be a miniature FM transceiver. So I tossed it in a closet. A minute later, somebody yelled "Raid!" Hah. Bug out. Then Swazey came in and told me I should put it back in the window to keep the burglars away. I put it back.

***

Around this time Bill Timm called up: "Jim, ahem, listen closely now, ahem, and make sure you ahem, understand what I'm, ahem, really saying."

He really said "Ahem." Ahaw.

"We're taking you off the payroll."

"I, ahem, understand, Bill." (Once off that payroll, on to Ling-Temco-Vought's or whatever subsidiary or formality, I figured, or out to Seattle. But good to know I had been getting paid for all of this.)

"Jim, I've also arranged to pay for your life insurance out of my own pocket."

"Why, thank you, Bill. That's very kind of you, sir." (Since I had no dependents and a fair life expectancy at 22, like, so what? Nice gesture, but — or nice, unless.... What's the, ahem, point here?)

***

Everywhere I walked to the cadence of "LOOK BEFORE BACKING," chanting in my mind at the very edge of aloud. On a wind-driven rainy night I went to get a paper at the newsstand on Broadway, walking in on the proprietor's quickie market report: "Went up, went down, but came all the way back up again." On the way out, someone said, "This ought to be easy. He just has to walk around his — "

His ZIP code. 10027. Up, down, all the way back up again: to the upper border, 125$^{\underline{th}}$ Street, up the long steep stone stairs into Riverside Park, down through fifteen soaking blocks, staggering in the crosswind off the river, tacking up and east, trailing the backup-lit cars, then blown along Cathedral Parkway, W. 110th, maybe the windiest street in Manhattan, to the lee of Amsterdam Avenue, past St. John's and the Cathedral Station Post Office (10025), then around and back up, if nothing else, keeping the newspaper dry. Neither rain nor....

***

When I walked past garages, sometimes the red neon would just show

PAR, but if I were doing well, the sign would light up

KING.

***

At 380 Riverside Drive in Leslee's apartment one night there was a strange candlelit meeting. She sat me down in the easy chair and gave me a glass of milk and a plate of cookies. Silently, a dozen or more people came in: I thought I recognized them, maybe, in little light, with no glasses, but their hair was longer or they were dressed differently. Somebody sprayed Silly String all over me, binding me softly to the chair. Leslee and her roommates read lengthy horoscopes aloud: I swear every one was about me. Then everyone gathered in the middle of the living room, sent up puffs of smoke, and dispersed.

"There was something in that cookie," I murmured as the walk back home seemed to go on endlessly, past the great gracious houses above the paths deep in the dense park along the river rippling with waves of reflected light.

***

I had been down in the dumps, the furniture and appliance potter's fields under the arching, rattling iron of the West Side Highway viaduct. Then I wandered toward the river, onto a service road marked with a city sign:

PLOW DOWN

I thrilled to think of Hopkins: "…sheer plod makes plough down sillion shine," and the grand Pare Lorentz documentary, "The Plow That Broke The Plains."

***

I stopped short at an old familiar forbidding sign at the foot of a block perpendicular to Riverside Drive and the park:

NO COMMERCIAL TRAFFIC

Directly above, the rear of an equestrian statue, and right in line with the equine tail, a red traffic warning light. O. Commercial traffic? Horse's ass. *You're* not commercial.

On the riverbank along the Henry Hudson Parkway, with river rats the size of spaniels, the same sign, with "NO" obscured by a bumper sticker:

SPIRIT OF FLESH.

***

121

Behind Grant's Tomb, at the head of the memorial Defender Grove of elms, enclosed by a tall iron fence is a solitary skinny crooked tree, an 1897 gift of the Government of China. Down to the smallest tortuous branch, it is the very model and image of the tree illustrated in my "COME TO MIDDLE EARTH" poster.

Is this where I am?

***

Early one morning I walked through the cold courtyard of International House, Sakura Park, stopping to look at a large cement multistory pagoda birdhouse. Straight up very far in the clear sky, an airplane headed toward the Island and the Atlantic, another in parallel proceeded toward the Palisades and Jersey. I see. One flew east, one flew west, and one flew over the cuckoo's nest.

***

Seeking asylum

The Friday night came when I ran out of food — *really* ran out, past fossils trapped in freezer snow, even beyond ketchup, salad dressing, and steak sauce, which had served as side dishes if not full meals. No problem, except that I had also run out of money…and patience, perseverance, fortitude, faith, hope, and time.

Andy Bronin called up. I saw Andy very occasionally, and wasn't even sure I much cared for him, but he had called once before recently, and now repeated his offer: "Are you feeling alright? You wanna go to Lukie's?"

St. Luke's Hospital, home of the Columbia University Psychiatric Service, and a rest stop for many people I knew, mostly with acute caffeine psychosis, girlfriend/ boyfriend problems, no-girlfriend/-boyfriend problems, roommate problems, midterms, papers, finals, culture shock, *kulturkampf*, general malaise, *mal de siècle*, *mal de mer*, *mal'occhio*, malingering, acute *Zeitgeist,* chronic *angst* or generalized *sturm und drang.* Or all of the above.

Andy was a post-BA pre-med: he needed the clinical experience, so I agreed. "Might need to do that. Yeah. Sounds like a good idea. Might help."

He came right up in a cab and we took the subway to St. Luke's. My first visit to this or any emergency room: here, a lot of perfectly well-looking, well-behaved people waiting and acting like automata. Andy proceeded to study his organic chemistry, pacing in well-defined patterns. I noted signs advising of a $13.00 charge for the visit — but if I'm not really sick, that doesn't really apply.

After not too long I was interviewed, with Andy supplying most of the details. I had to furnish my mother's maiden name. Which I did. "That's a killer," the clerk says. Andy grimaced.

<<Wha? I'm supposed to be deceptive *here* too?>>

Then I was taken to sit on a table in a treatment room with all sorts of serious stuff in the chrome and glass wall cabinets — tracheotomy kit, respirator, IV bags, and a whole Craftsman® tool set of fearsome stainless instruments. Everything here is an object lesson in "LOOK BEFORE BACKING." Also a statement of perspective: your case doesn't warrant this. This isn't an emergency. Your life is not in jeopardy. You just need something to eat.

Before long a young physician came in wearing a tie with a pattern that looked like Tenneco logos. He in turn sent in a Dr. Diaz in a green raincoat, who asked me if I wanted drugs. I knew better than to flat-out ask. "I don't know. Only if you think they're needed." He asked if I were hearing voices. I knew that hearing voices was dead-bang loony, so I presented with alienation and *anomie*:

"Doctor, I find that I have become reclusive, and have lost touch with people, and people seem to be avoiding me. I seem to be losing track of what's happening, and I'm not sure what to do next....": three-minute monolog of misery.

No sooner did I finish than he stepped outside and very audibly ordered eight Thorazine®. Had no idea I was that convincing. "I usually don't prescribe these to outpatients, but they should help you," he said. "Take two tonight before bed and call me tomorrow." I was given eight dull red tablets in a small plain brown envelope — no imprint, no patient or physician name, no directions, no precautions, just a casually handwritten "Thorazine."

Andy then hiked me down fifteen blocks to his apartment, where he invited me to fix myself a sandwich. Baloney and white bread. Golly. He's actually offering me *meat*.

Throughout, Andy was drilling doubletime back and forth, marching stiffly, cornering sharply, which reminded me of the way I was backing and forthing in my apartment. When I put the knife on top of the Miracle Whip® jar he had a conniption. On my way out he lent me $2.00 (and made a point of collecting some time later.) $2.00 in retrospect seems cheap, but sufficient for my purposes then, and most welcome.

I hustled up through the horizontal snow, halfway along stopping at the usual all-night market to buy bread and margarine. Upon arriving uptown, from a nearby apartment I heard someone laughing, "It's a placebo. It's only *aspirin*." I wouldn't know Thorazine (chlorpromazine HCl, SK&F) if I OD'd on it. After I gorged on toast, I examined the pills. Under the red M&M coating was a white tablet with the taste of aspirin. I took two: they had the same effect as aspirin, but I did sleep well.

Dr. Diaz called the next day, and I told him I was fine, thank you very much. "Did the medication help?"

124

"It was aspirin, doctor, not Thorazine."

"Did it help you sleep?"

"Well, yes it did."

"You should come in again."

"I'm fine, doctor. Thank you."

Next, a call from another doctor who seemed to rank: he sounded both official and insistent, so I agreed to see him. He may have also sounded like Don Booth. On the way to the appointment, I smelled smoke and saw a Volkswagen stripped and smoldering. "Burnt folks," I thought. That sounded like Judy.

At St. Luke's I was sent right up to the doctor's office. He smoked KENT® (with the Micronite™ Filter — "Thinking man's filter, smoking man's taste") and kept blowing smoke in my face. Mostly he asked about my background, which I furnished accurately but generally, and that's that. Come to think of, he sorta looked like Don Booth.

A few afternoons later that doctor called again and suggested — urged — that I make another appointment.

"Excuse me, doctor, but have you had lunch today?"

"Why yes, of course. Why do you ask?"

"I would respectfully suggest, doctor, that you are in your CUPS*."

"Very well then."

***

Meantime I did not have to subsist on the change from Andy Bronin's $2, having either cashed a check or come across a forgotten fin or sawbuck in a pocket ("I live in a silver mine and I call it 'beggar's tomb'" — The Grateful Dead.) So the next day at the all-night market I got bread, margarine, and, on impulse, from a display box right up on the counter, a bar of Joyva® Halvah. The cash register rang up $1.44. The clerk said "Now you know how to square a circle." Halvah: crushed sesame seeds.

***

---

* Columbia University Psychiatric Services. Among the longest joke setups ever recorded: I first used the line in a *Jester* story five years earlier. Not that I ever thought that doctors lunched like admen. Not even shrinks.

125

For whatever reason — Swazey may have encouraged it — I decided to go visit the Agency. Putting on my green Macy's raglan-sleeve raincoat, I said (apologies to Joe Penner), "I wanna buy a Doc."

Down at the shop, I found Vinnie and Mark, who began to make some stagey phone calls. Then both of them walked out with me stooped deep in my raincoat. Vinnie said "We're getting him some help" to Fred Yosca, the office manager, as I mumbled assent.

<<How to simulate mental illness: just disengage...disconnect...dis-integrate. Play along. Stick to the script, shoot the storyboard.>>

They took me in a cab up to St. Luke's, where Dr. Diaz-Montos talked to Vinnie, made a call, sent us downtown. Slumped in the back of another cab, I tried not to look out at the river from the FDR Drive, all the way straight down to Bellevue.

<<Bellevue? *Bellevue!*>>

Bellevue: directed from one old brick building to another, in and out, all over the campus and back — another in a series of appointed runarounds. Certainly. What did I expect? They keep keeping things interesting. Finally the right place, through a hallway heavy with cops, two of them guarding this sorry specimen named Jason in seersucker pajamas. At the door to Jason's room, the officers were kicking around a rectangular piece of paper the size of a cigarette butt, which he was following intently, crawling around and stalking, nearly but not quite springing and pouncing. Rather like me scrabbling and scrounging for smokes. Across the hall, an authoritative-looking well-dressed guy sat on a bench and smoked extravagantly.

Up at the desk, I gave my mother's wrong maiden name, my religion as Protestant, and my birthdate in error, not to mention every other detail I could fib or fuzz. All this served either to conceal my true identity or demonstrate real confusion with the facts, which might have been the point anyway.

Initially I was interviewed by a white-coated young man who had what I thought could have been ECT gear — a box with switches, lights, and a pair of heavy duty jumper cable electrodes. As I answered each question about my history and symptoms, a bell or a buzzer would go off: could have been the phone or the intercom, but it seemed like some sorta lie detector. Give the wrong answer and get a shock. Apparently I passed.

We then went to wait in a TV room full of other inmates. Vinnie was talking to someone in the hall, Mark sat down at my right. On my left, I saw a guy in profile resembling my brother, declaiming incomprehensibly in my brother's junkie yawny drawl. Looking at the TV, which was showing nifty SST footage, I saw that with every move I made, right or left, forward or back, up or down, port open or closed*, the TV picture responded as a mirror.

A nurse said she was giving me a shot to calm my nerves. I rolled up my sleeve and clenched my fist for a hit in the mainline, but she put it in my shoulder. Into the TV room came a tall bald man pushing a thin grey-haired woman in a wheelchair. I could only see their backs, and heard the woman say "Does he know that I'm here?"

The last time I saw my mother, terminal with metastatic carcinoma of the lung, was in that very same scene. At this I was expressionless. All I felt was "Cheap shot, jagoffs. Nice try. You gotta do a lot better than that."

Then I was sent to a huge shower room to strip, turn over my clothes and my glasses, and dress in seersucker pajamas secured at the waist by a gauzy string, topped by a thin blue poplin robe, with paper and rubber slippers. No cavity search, no delousing, not even a mandatory shower, and the attendant was pleasantly, respectfully polite. So far, so good. I got on a gurney for the ride upstairs.

***

---

* "Close your porthole" — mandatory body language nuance: never expose private parts, front or rear. Always sit with legs crossed or hands clasped in lap; standing, join cupped hands behind asshole.

Total commitment

The double doors open onto Ward No. 5.

THIS, FOR ALL I CAN SEE, IS THE SCARIEST MOMENT OF MY LIFE.

This is bedlam. This is crazy. People wandering all around in nothing but noise.

Sign on the wall says

PUPPET SHOW!

APRIL 10

Admission FREE!

OK, Vinnie. Serves me right for swiping the Gronk mockup. I get the point. Great joke. Ya really got me this time. Hahaha. Alright. Joke's over. Seriously. I'm not kidding. Fun's fun. Hey, c'mon, guys. Get me *outta* here.

C'mon. Shit. Enough already.

On a locker above some cardplayers is another sign:

Coffee Bar

CIGARETTES

45¢ to patients 55¢ to visitors

I don't have the price of a square of smokes, so I sit down next to a tray of green apples and ask a smoking geezer if I can have one of his. No. OK.

This place is full of wackos, from fat to fasting, geriatric to adolescent, slovenly to natty, out-of-it to out of control, warped every which way, a mental menagerie, a zoo of zanies, maybe 30 or 40 in all, all cogwheeling around, acting out.

I start walking with them. I'm here. We're all in this together, together through sick and sin. There is this frail girl named Candy who is being flung around the dining room and up and down the hall through a gauntlet of yelling and slapping. I catch her on a rebound.

"Candy, why are they doing this?"

"[Mumblegarblegobbledegook]."

"Candy, who are you?"

"I'm a spirit." She smiles reassuringly. She may be my surrogate.

It's late. I'm tired. Enough: this isn't fun anymore. I find a bed and rack out, expecting to be roused into deliverance. Vinnie and Mark will come by any minute now to get me out of bed, out of here. No such luck. A nurse wakes me up and tells me nicely that this isn't my bed. "New patient beds are in the hall so we can watch over them."

The next morning in the hall I get breakfast in bed: orange juice, coffee, toast, all in bowls, no utensils. Nobody came for me. But I do get my glasses back, with my name in adhesive tape on an earpiece.

***

Ward No. 5 is a U-shape, men in rooms in the right ascender, women on the left leg, topped by a spacious sunny group meeting room. Across the bottom are doctors' offices, exam rooms, the nurses' station with a Dutch door for the medication queues, the dining room/day room with an always-on TV[*], and the locked double doors leading to locked elevators. The windows have heavy screens, but I can see a street and some old brick houses right below my corner, and twenty blocks straight uptown, the Empire State Building shining at night.

The first patient I get to know is Mr. Mandy, my roommate, a mild, moon-faced, serene gent. Just the two of us in a bay with some ten beds — semi-private, which is perfectly fine by me.

The coffee bar is run by wiry smirky cardplaying guys with ageless DA haircuts, Mr. Sharkey and Mr. Toohey, often joined by a slatternly shower-shod lady named Irene. There is Donna, a very large gal with breasts like basketballs. Donna is an Indian elephant with a counterpart, an equally big broad who more resembles an African elephant. In the Simon and Garfunkel bestiary, "The elephants are kindly but they're dumb." Then there is a pig, a homely girl with unkempt frizzy red blonde hair, her pajama top tied up under her small droopy tits. She keeps calling me "Darling."

---

[*] Try watching a candy bar commercial when half-starved and abstinent from candy for months. I cannot forget the spot for "Rally" candy bars, which may have flopped as a new product — no longer on the market — but which I had to buy as soon as I got out. Irresistible. The power of advertising.

Ward No. 5 is also home to some very old gentlemen in wheelchairs, a few shuffling elderly women, a number of nondescript kids, big black doc, blonde lady doc, blonde nursie, cheery hunchback therapist, and a kid social worker with a standard New-York-superior attitude. And Candy. And myself.

***

Never having been in a psychiatric hospital[*] before, I have no idea what to expect in terms of treatment. The first morning, an interview with a lady doc: I am trying hard, but not overtrying, to come across as normal, stable, rational, responsible, respectable, realistic. Surely it's obvious that I'm not in the same condition as the rest of these folks. Clearly I don't belong here of all places.

<<Like I was going to really 'fess up to what was happening. *As if.* "Well, doctor, it's a long story. A funny thing happened to me on my way to Bellevue. First I threw my keys and wallet into a mailbox to help qualify for some new business at the ad agency where I worked. Then this black dude made the subway train come by hitting the platform twice with his stick. The next day, I thought I was going to California, but I couldn't cross my block because sheets of ice fell at the corners. So I walked around, surrounded by all these classic cars, and following passing conversations I was meant to overhear. The signposts moved up and down on Park Avenue. I'm sure you're aware of Jim Ling, the Cowboy's Cabs, and the principles of "LOOK BEFORE BACKING." Well, as you'd expect, there were lots of rattletraps riding around. That night, the whole city lit up with the pictures from the walls of my apartment — even a caricature of me, in profile, which, as you can see, is not my best side. I have been secluded, in training, Ranger-style negative motivation, directed by the radio, voices in the hall, and a blind ex-cop in drag as a WWI army nurse. I believed that if I crossed the street the wrong way, Riverside Church would fall on me. And I've spent several nights

---

[*] Or any hospital since a tonsillectomy at age 5, when I was told that Dr. Kaczynski, the family G.P., would award a cowboy suit to whichever patient drank the most water post-op. A Great Lake later, after contant inquiries, I was informed that Little Bobby Kaminski won the suit. He in turn heard that I had won. Inevitably, eventually we compared notes. Little Bobby grew up to become a society gynecologist, forsaking earlier aspirations to the priesthood. We both became realists.

just riding the subways. Did I mention that I live on Sesame Street?>>

<<Like, sure. They'd throw away the key. I'd end up wearing seersucker out of season, and a 60-long canvas jacket that would not pass for hopsack.>>

I therefore said very little at some length. The smalltalking cure. I may be a little neurotic, but who isn't these days? I feel pretty well. I'm OK, you're OK. Why am I here? Some friends thought I was becoming distant and withdrawn, but I was just trying to avoid them. I appreciated their good intentions, so I went along for the ride. But obviously I'm not a danger to myself or society, even in New York City. I mean, really. These are *advertising* people. What do they know?

I also expect that any second, the doc is going to disclose that it was all a prank.

Then there is group therapy. We all convene in a big circle session which seems to be both patient parliament and semi-coherent self-criticism. I sit through this stolidly, despite the nudging presence of the piggy girl, who has ensconced herself right next to me. At the end of the session, when most everyone has left, she plants her hand on my pajamaed, unbriefed crotch.

"Darling...."

"Get the hell outta there. That's private."

Later that day I wake up from a nap to find her leaning over my bed. Mr. Mandy told her to get lost. Said she was odd that way. I tell him, "Hey, man, I wouldn't fuck her with *your* dick."

Apropos of modesty, I am having trouble with the hospital-issued clothing. The pants are big in the waist, with no hips to hang on. They always feel like they are about to fall down, or the flimsy gauze cincture is about to come undone. In the tub room I find a sheaf of gauze ties, so I wrap them several of them together, pull them tight, knot and double knot. After a few days I am allowed to wear my street clothes (herringbone jacket, pastel green shirt, maroon polka dot tie) on the ward, but one of the cinctures will not unknot, so I have a reminder tied around my belly.

In the hall I sneak a peek through the wire glass into the mattress-lined isolation ("quarantine") room, newly occupied. The scrawny scuzzy bearded fella inside signs that he needs some water, which I get right away from the bathroom, only to find the heavy wooden door unshakably locked. An aide asks, "How do you think you'd feel in one of those?" <<Kinda like being in a mailbox, huh?>> "You'd probably feel just — rotten," I allowed.

Four times a day we line up for medication. The shots of Donald Duck pink grapefruit juice are tasty, but the meds are translucent gel spheres and footballs that don't do a thing for me. No ups, no downs, no sharps, no flats, no mellow, no nothing. *Nada.* Placebos. Bummer. My first chance to try antipsychotics and major tranks, and I am getting USP Jujubes®.

Eventually I have to sit down with the full-of-himself kid therapist for a reality test. At least I can ace this one. Name, address, occupation, education, month and year, current location, a little verbal sport explaining metaphors and interpreting proverbs (HINT: if you're ever in a similar situation, they evidently always use the same ones — *"A stitch in time saves nine." "A rolling stone gathers no moss." "One man's meat is another man's poison"* — although they could have stumped me with *"What's good for the goose is sauce for the gander."*) C'mon, gimme some inkblots, a maze, "What's wrong with this picture?", or at least a little word association. Even some round pegs and square holes. Then, toward the end, "Name the last three presidents of the United States."

"President Nixon, President Johnson, President Kennedy, and President Eisenhower."

"I asked you to name three and you named four. Why?"

"Because I have no particular taste for President Nixon."

A little while later I go to the bathroom, sit in a stall, and read on the door in Magic Marker,

What are you trying to do —

stink up the place?

No shit!!!!

Nixon's the One!

***

To me the most efficacious treatment is food therapy. After breakfast and lunch in bed, I am permitted to join the dinner crowd,

132

which begins forming up well ahead of time until one of the staff announces "Truck's up!" to herald the arrival of the stainless steel steam cart. Then we advance on the cart, snatch trays and utensils, plates and cups and bowls, hold them out to be filled, and sit down quick to eat.

These people have the most godawful atrocious table manners I have ever seen. Real animals, eating with their hands, slurping off the trays, cramming stuff into their mouths with stuff hanging out, food all over their faces, slopping and spilling all over the table and the floor and themselves, grunting, chomping, chewing and yumming loudly and constantly from the first bite through the last lick of dessert.

At this point I am prepared to eat anything and like it. But the food is remarkably good here at Bellevue — better in fact than in the University dining halls and many upper Broadway restaurants, good enough to have been catered. I am feeling better with every meal. In fact, the first time I am allowed to handle utensils, I am encouraged that someone points out to me the words stamped into the flatware:

PROPERTY OF
THE CITY OF NEW YORK.

So indeed I am.

Nightly they call us for "Nourishment, ladies and gentlemen." Peanut butter and jelly sandwiches and milk. Hey, I ain't picky. A patient points to the puddle beneath the food cart and asks what it is. "Spilled milk. Don't cry over it." For one snack we get a sheet cake, but the moment I arrive, the piggy girl snatches the last piece and mashes it into her mouth. "Hey. You take the cake."

During that nourishment, Candy appears in the hall with a beat-up umbrella, opens it above her head and chants from Buffy Ste.-Marie,

Little wheel, spin and spin;
Big wheel turn around and around.

On my way to a meal, Candy comes up to me outside the men's washroom, holding up a cloth as if to wipe my face *à la* St. Veronica:

"My sweet Lord!"

"I'm nobody's Lord, Candy."

"Then wash up."

Quick turn into the bathroom. *"Lavabo inter innocentes manus meus,"* I recite. *I will wash my hands among the innocent.*

***

The piggy girl brings a *Good Housekeeping* magazine over to me and opens it to an ad for Campbell's Soup, Chicken with Stars:

TWINKLE, TWINKLE, BRIGHTER STARS.

***

From the first day of the stay I come across graffiti that keep the spirit company. At the nurses' station:

Bellevue.

Thorazine® is *good.*

Friends' names carved into the corkboards, and a note pointing up to my bedroom,

→ This way is ~~North~~ West →.

Go rest, young man.

After several days, as I begin to think I have been marooned here, on the quarantine room door, a line from a Steppenwolf song:

AMERICA, WHERE ARE YOU NOW?

Simultaneously, from Scripture:

Eloi, eloi, lama sabacthani?

"My God, my God, why hast Thou forsaken me?" But I never felt forsaken, least of all by my God.

***

I do get visitors. Old Mark brings along Annapurna, my continuously erstwhile Barnard girlfriend. As we are chatting, suddenly I think I am divulging privileged information, so I clam up. Half-seriously, I wonder aloud if Annapurna could smuggle me out in the folds of her sari.

"Haha. Just kidding."

"Not even if I wore a 9-yard sari."

"You'd look real pregnant."

"I'd look like a float."

"Hey, Wiz, you're sure you're not just horny?"

"Hey, Mark, with all these crazy chicks in pajamas around here?"

Finally I give Mark my apartment keys so he can retrieve my mail and make sure that everything is more or less, heaven forfend, the way I left it.

134

Nat Wander — anthropology major dubbed "El Groundhog" back at Stuyvesant High in Brooklyn — and Randy Mound — pre-med self-styled "Captain Love" during our fleeting hippie phase — come by in a couple days with the keys and the mail. Included are my final SSCandB paychecks and a lump sum distribution of my profit-sharing account, altogether a nice piece of change, which I endorse for Nat to deposit.

While we are going through the papers they are generously sharing smokes, Camel Filters ("They're not for everybody.") The cigarettes give me a prop to handle furtively while talking out of the side of my mouth in a stock prison-visiting-room *shtick*. Randy has a foam cup of the thin sour ward coffee, and he is breaking □ □ □ □ □ pieces off the top, methodically all the way around, until the cup looks like a crown.

***

Mr. Mandy keeps complaining to me about somebody on the staff: "He's into your personal things." Big deal: the only personal thing I care about is my raincoat, which I can see hanging up on a coatrack in a locked room. Obviously outerwear is not necessary for inpatients, but I think I may find it useful eventually. "He's into your personal things." Oh. I get it. Mark had my apartment keys. My place has been tossed. But what do I have to hide anyway? Even my journal notebooks, recording everything I've done and felt since the middle of high school: nahhh. Who could read the handwriting?

The next time I come back in the bay Mr. Mandy is taking a nap, his sweater off, laid across his shoulders and draped up around his head. Omigod. Cowl ling.

Cowl ling. The sweater is even the same color brown as the habit of the Order of Friars Minor Capuchin Franciscans. Mr. Mandy is Father Mandy, O.F.M. Cap. *He* was into my personal things. I do believe that on Ward No.5 at Bellevue Hospital in March, 1971 I received a general absolution of all my sins.

***

One morning I wake up and above my bed, drawn a foot high in red and blue:

135

U ✪ S.

"Next day on your dressing room, they've hung a star/Let's go on with the show."

In the next bed is the beardo who had been in quarantine. He gets up, leaving on his pillow a nickel, some pennies, and a fat gooey booger. Mr. Mandy looks and shakes his head. I recollect a line from the cover of James Simon Kunen's *The Strawberry Statement*, which I had presented to Don Booth to reciprocate for his passalong of James Dickey's *Deliverance*. "Society may think we are all snot-nosed brats," or some such to that effect.

That night I can't find an empty seat at dinner, so later I make a meal of peanut butter and jelly, also guzzling coffee because it feels like something is up. Up north, the Empire State Building beacon, spire, and topmost stories are dark. Flying over the hospital building across the way, the American flag flutters in shreds. I immediately think of a *Jester* editor and unlikely NROTC cadet, nearly as funny in person and in writing as his name would be for a naval officer: "I'll tear your tattered ensign down, Jupa."

On the table near my bed have been placed three cups of cold coffee. Outside, three matched trailer trucks snarl past together. "Trinity," I say to myself.

At the table is a chair marked "OT Dept." Overtime. Got it. I begin scurrying all around the wing, from the tub room to quarantine to the bathroom and back, keeping moving, staying stealthy until 3 a.m., when I stick my head out into the center room and ask the nurse on duty what time it is. Then I rack out. There is a dream with a final message: "DON'T CHOO IN BED."

I awaken that morning to find another graffito above my bed, in green:

⊛UT.

***

Around lunchtime I work my way into the ward office to find a phone, within earshot of the African elephant in the next room braying "Jewess!" into the phone. OK, Judy, I'll give her a hard disapproving look just for you. Then I call my office, get my (former) secretary, the ethereal Fran Peace, known to go braless with translucent blouses, subject of too many "Peace movement" lines, and I tell Fran that I will be on my way up there to visit sometime today.

(My only previous escape attempt failed. That caper came during a ward cookie sale, for which I had made "CHOCOLATE CHIP COOKIE" signs with little brown chips in the "O"s, applying years of creative consumer advertising experience.

(Throughout the sale, people were coming and going through the ward doors, so I sidled up next to a bunch, timed the automatic closer, and the next time nobody was looking, slipped through at the closing and out into the elevator lobby. The elevator was locked, but all I needed was the next carload of people to get off and then....

(Then an aide came out and told me I was not supposed to be out there. I told him I got lost.)

After lunch, unbeknownst to me in advance, a select group gets to go upstairs to Occupational Therapy, a/k/a Arts and Crafts: such a useful way to occupy oneself. The therapist, Miss Pippos, shepherds a load of us up to the 10$\underline{th}$ floor, the elevator doors opening on glimpses of other floors, signed with high-powered labels like "Nuclear Medicine Dept." and "Tropical Diseases — Enteric Fever Section."

Up in OT, I am given a candystriped coat with a "Volunteer" tag. "Volunteers of America, got to revolution," the Jefferson Airplane exhorts through my head.

We get to play with clay. How...folk artsy. I build a vase that begins to look like a toilet bowl with an "H" at the base. Nahhh. All I need is for them to think I am anal. So I modify the shape to something squatter, and decorate it all around with pseudo-primitive waves, Morse code, and Ugaritic glyphs.

One of the OT aides says to me, "You know how to use tools." I feel like taking the wire and wood whatsis instrument I was using and flinging it into the air like the ape in *2001*.

From the portable radio on the counter, the Plastic Ono Band, very loud:

> Power to the people, power to the people,
> Power to the people, right on!

We wash our hands and our tools and go out to the elevator for Miss Pippos to take us back down to Ward No. 5. "Aha," I say aloud to myself. "Miss Pippos passes."

Entering the elevator, I worm my way into a corner at the back, where several other passengers shift to close ranks in front of me. The elevator stops at Ward No. 5. Miss Pippos and the patients get off, I scroonch down deep inside the corner, the folks screening me move tighter together.

The doors stay open for a dreadful suspenseful long time. Miss Pippos pokes her head back in. "Ward No. 5, anybody else?", she calls. No answer. I stay on. The doors close. On the fourth floor, security guards get on, but they seem benign.

At the ground floor I stay hunched down in the pocket of people getting off. They peel away, I glance all around, then turn hard left and out the door to the parking lot, where a sign says "SOUND HORN."

Once out of the gate I start marching through the clear cold afternoon, thirty blocks up and three avenues over, flanked by an escort of the Cowboy's cabs in constant persevering procession.

***

To 575 Lexington, 15$^{\underline{th}}$ floor. On Don Booth's door, a Magic Markered sketchpad sign: "WELCOME BACK." In the background, I hear "Didja hear what Bill did?"

I work my way through a gauntlet of greetings back to my office. On my desk, the new issue of FORTUNE, cover headed

NEW YORK HANGS OUT THE "FOR-RENT" SIGN

Got that.

My stuff has been packed in boxes, which I have to root through to find what I want — sample packages of Lipton Main Dishes, my short-term menu plan. The office manager drops by, asks about my health. I ask if I might put some of my stuff in a bag and take it home. He says for that he would have to get me a pass, which would be a nuisance, and he'll have the whole load delivered in a few days anyway. "Mind if I take my clipboard? Don't need a pass for that, do I?"

"Go right ahead. I guess it's OK. It *is* your clipboard, isn't it? Not the Agency's?"

"Actually, it's Uncle Sam's, Fred. World War II memento." I flip it to the back to show the worn laminated wood neatly lettered:

CAPT. C.F. WISNIEWSKI, D.C.

O - 1726030.

Into my pockets I stuff the envelopes of noodles and sauce from Lipton Beef Stroganoff and Ham Cheddarton — and can't forget a brace of my medium point Bic® pens, my preference over the Agency-standard-issue writer's-cramp-inducing Accountant Fine Points.

Uptown in the black building the same light is still burning in the same window.

***

The Big Idea

I cannot think without a pen and a clipboard, so as soon as I got them back I got down to (free, speculative, unsolicited, unassigned) work. The front end here is wholly hypothetical, cut from whole cloth, reconstructed from memory, presented in typical agency proposal format. The advertising comes straight off the clipboard.

The inspiration came from one of those "Greatest Ads Ever Done, Never Run." It seemed that NASA used Lysol® Spray Disinfectant to sanitize the Apollo 11 astronauts' snakeskin boots, to help prevent contamination of the moon by earth organisms and vice versa. The Client was then running a full-page color ad in LIFE, "Lysol Spray helps you get away this summer" — away from odors, germs, etc. I suggested a facing page, black-and-white — footprint in the lunar dust, "Lysol Spray helped Neil Armstrong get away this summer." The ad got bought, then scrubbed. The closest I got to the mission was admiring the actual-size LEM on display outside the TIME-LIFE building, and watching the landing telecast in Central Park.

The idea had come to mind at the outset of the training, if not before. All I needed was to put it down and fill it out.

Background

[There was no FedEx then, no Purolator, no Courier Express. Messengers rode shoe leather, not bikes. United Parcel had no consumer franchise. Airborne was a freight forwarder. DHL was somebody's monogram. The Railway Express Agency had begun aggressive competitive marketing with silver trucks, a Western motif, and the slogan "Hi-Yo, R-E-A, away!", which they even used in answering their phones. In this context....] The U.S. Post Office is at best taken for granted as not only a legal monopoly but a traditional, historical, political American institution. At worst it may at times be perceived to be slow, unreliable, inefficient, bureaucratic, resistant to change, and unresponsive to patrons' needs. The letter carriers' strike has added to negative perceptions. Postal reorganization appears to be a sound approach in theory, but remains to be proven in practice. To patrons at large, whose awareness of reorganization is minimal, the Postal Service may well be the same old Post Office doing business as usual.

The challenge is to change all those perceptions. The obligation is massive. The opportunity is unprecedented.

Objectives

Establish the new identity and status of the United States Postal Service...

...and demonstrate its unique strengths in terms of scope, speed, security,

and economy...

...among consumer, corporate, and Postal Service employee audiences, as well as legislative and other governmental influences...

...and to increase branch traffic, awareness, and trial of postal services...

...in a six-month initial period beginning July 1, 1971.

Strategy

Identify the Postal Service with the most advanced, most powerful and boldly successful venture in U.S. history, and dramatize USPS capabilities through direct, active, essential involvement in that venture.

<u>Tactics</u>

1. Secure the cooperation of the National Aeronautics and Space Administration in designating an upcoming Apollo moon mission as

THE U.S. MAIL,

and accordingly, naming the Apollo spacecraft modules

THE WABASH CANNONBALL (Command Module)
THE YANKEE CLIPPER (Service Module)
THE SPIRIT OF ST. LOUIS (Lunar Module)

for the modes of transportation that carry the mail;

2. Obtain lunar samples and deliver them, via standard 1st Class mail, to post office branches throughout the country for public exhibition, as well as to a select group of governmental and opinion leaders and mass mailers;

(Not coincidentally, for NASA's benefit, this would stimulate public interest in the space program. Further, it would literally deliver compelling physical proof of the results of the public's massive investment in space.)

3. Amplify the identification and image through intensive promotion, publicity, and point-of-sale merchandising tie-ins;

4. To reinforce the message, introduce and seat a corporate slogan, and augment the image, secure exclusive use of the hit song "Don't Mess With The U.S. Mail" as a jingle and tag line for universal application.

James Casimir Wisniewski

"DELIVERY"

VIDEO	AUDIO
1. ANIMATION: OPEN ON LS APOLLO SPACECRAFT EMERGING AT HIGH SPEED FROM BEHIND MOON	MUSIC: JINGLE RHYTHM TRACK CAPCOM (V.O.): Apollo 15, you are GO for lunar landing.... (FADE RADIO TRAFFIC, TELEMETRY UNDER)
2. ZOOM IN ON APPROACH-ING SPACECRAFT MODULES	ANNCR (V.O.): Anyone can promise you the moon. Only we can deliver.
3. ZOOM IN, SEE MOON IN BG.	The moon's coming down to earth —
4. PUSH IN ON USPS LOGO ON SPACECRAFT	brought to you by the new United States Postal Service:
5. PAN TO NAME ON COMMAND MODULE	The Wabash Cannonball,
6. PAN TO NAME ON SERVICE MODULE	The Yankee Clipper,
7. LUNAR LANDER UN-DOCKING, DESCENDING; PUSH IN ON NAME	and the Spirit of St. Louis —
8. PULL BACK	the trains and boats and planes that bring you
9. SWOOSH ON LOGO, EARTH AND MOON IN BG	(JINGLE UP) the U.S. Mail.
10. MATCH CUT SEQUENCE TO LOGO ON AIRCRAFT, VEHICLES, UNIFORMS, MAILBOXES, BRANCHES	The new U.S. Postal Service: six hundred thousand people... forty thousand post offices...the biggest civilian fleet of vehicles in the world,
11. CONTINUE JUMPCUTS: BAGS, BOXES, LETTERS,	delivering billions of items to hundreds of millions of people —

144

SERVICE SCENES

12. DISS TO LUNAR DISPLAY IN LOCAL BRANCH	and now, delivering the moon by first class mail to a post office near you. (JINGLE UP)
13. DISS TO CANNONBALL REENTRY	The moon — brought to you by the biggest, fastest, farthest, safest, surest delivery system in the world — and beyond.
14. SWOOSH ON LOGO	(SFX: TELEMETRY UP)
	ASTRONAUT (V.O.): Don't mess with the U.S. Mail!
	SINGER (V.O.): Don't mess with the U.S. Mail!

James Casimir Wisniewski

U.S. Postal Service
Institutional Intro
:15 TV

"COMING SOON"

VIDEO	**AUDIO**
1. ANIMATION: APOLLO SPACECRAFT EMERGING FROM BEHIND MOON	SFX: RADIO, TELEMETRY UP AND UNDER MUSIC: JINGLE UP AND UNDER THROUGHOUT ANNCR (V.O.): The moon:
2. PUSH IN TO SEE NAMES…	it's coming down to earth —
3. HIGHLIGHT LOGO	brought to you by the U.S. Mail — the new U.S. Postal Service.
4. DISS THROUGH LOGO TO LUNAR SURFACE AND SAMPLE	The moon! Lunar samples coming soon to a post office near you —
5. PULL BACK TO SEE DISPLAY	by first class mail, through the biggest, fastest, farthest, safest, surest delivery system in the world — and beyond.
6. SEE ASTRONAUT IN SPACE SUIT W/ LOGO, LETTER CARRIER IN UNIFORM AT DISPLAY	ASTRONAUT (D.V.): Don't mess with the U.S. Mail! SINGER (V.O.): Don't mess with the U.S. Mail!
	MUSIC UP
7. POP ON LOCAL DISPLAY INFO	
	MUSIC, SFX UP AND OUT

U.S. Postal Service
Institutional Intro
:15 TV

"BROUGHT TO YOU"

VIDEO	**AUDIO**
1. OPEN ON TELEPHOTO, FULL MOON	MUSIC: JINGLE UNDER THROUGH-OUT ANNCR (V.O.): The moon!.
2. ZOOM IN ON SURFACE	Coming soon —
3. PULL BACK TO SEE LUNAR SAMPLE IN CASE	to a post office near you!
4. PULL BACK, SEE CROWD	Lunar samples brought to you by first class mail by
5. SUPER USPS LOGO	the new United States Postal Service.
6. MATCH DISS TO LOGO ON APOLLO 15 SPACECRAFT	ASTRONAUT (V.O.): Don't mess with the U.S. Mail! SINGER (V.O.):Don't mess with the U.S. Mail! MUSIC: JINGLE UP AND OUT

U.S. Postal Service
Institutional Intro
:60 Radio

"U.S. MAIL"

SFX: NASA TELEMETRY, RADIO

JINGLE UP AND UNDER

ANNCR: America's bringing the moon home — and it's coming by first class mail — delivered by the new U.S. Postal Service aboard Apollo Fifteen — the Wabash Cannonball, the Yankee Clipper, and the Spirit of St. Louis, named for the trains, the boats, and the planes that carry the U.S. Mail.

JINGLE UP

There's a piece of the moon coming soon for you to see at a post office near you. Anybody can promise you the moon, but only the U.S. Mail can deliver it —

JINGLE UP

with six hundred thousand people working in forty thousand post offices, with the biggest civilian fleet of vehicles in the world — moving billions of pieces of mail to hundreds of millions of people.

JINGLE UP

Watch for the moon landing at a post office near you — brought to you by the biggest, fastest, farthest, safest, surest delivery system in the world — and beyond: the new U.S. Postal Service!

ASTRONAUT: Don't mess with the U.S. Mail!

SINGER: Don't mess with the U.S. Mail!

U.S. Postal Service
:30 Radio
Local Tie-in

"SEE IT"

JINGLE UP AND UNDER

LIVE ANNCR: You don't have to go to the moon to see it up close. The moon will be landing here in [OURTOWN] — a real lunar sample delivered by first class mail to POST OFFICE] at [ADDRESS]. See it on display from [DATE] to [DATE], [TIME A.M.] to [TIME P.M.] every day — brought to you by the new United States Postal Service.

JINGLE UP

SINGER: Don't mess with the U.S. Mail!

U.S. Postal Service
Institutional Intro Ad 2P4C

LEAD

The new United States Postal Service proudly introduces our newest delivery vehicle:

PIX

[Illustration: Airbrush rendering of Apollo 15 spacecraft modules]

HEADLINE

ANYBODY CAN PROMISE YOU THE MOON. ONLY WE CAN DELIVER IT

INTRO COPY

SUBHEADS

The moon is in the mail

Only 1st Class is good enough

The Apollo Program is worth billions. Postage costs pennies.

Mail to Moon Township, PA 15268...Jupiter, FL 61413...Pluto, NV 82345...Orion, KY 23456...and anywhere else on earth

Neither rain nor snow nor heat nor gloom of night shall stay these couriers from the swift completion of their appointed rounds.

CALLOUTS

[The Wabash Cannonball, The Yankee Clipper, The Spirit of St. Louis: spacecraft specs and related Postal Service facts and figures]

INSET PIX

[Sample loading, moonside...USPS pickup, Lunar Receiving Lab... samples *en route*...typical P.O. branch display]

FREE OFFER   For a poster-size print of this illustration, just visit your nearest Post Office branch.   But hurry. Supplies are limited, and they'll go like rockets.

BF CLOSE   **The biggest, fastest, farthest, safest, surest delivery system in the world — and beyond**

LOGO   [USPS]

TAG   **Don't mess with the U.S. Mail!**

***

James Casimir WHO?

That was the Prestype on the second sheet of my portfolio; first sheet, the full name. Now I could fill out an acronym…W…H…O:

✳Jimmy **W**alker, Hizzoner the Mayor, "Beau James," as portrayed in the movie by Bob Hope;

✳Jim **H**awkins of *Treasure Island*;

✳Jimmy **O**lsen, Superman's pal.

***

The minute I got back to the apartment I turned on the radio, and a few minutes later heard Neil Diamond's latest hit, "I Am, I Said" —

…and I am lost and I can't even say why….

During and after I held on tight to the bars on the window and wept in wonder.

***

["You're so vain, you prob'ly think this song is about you," Carly Simon, would not be released for several more months, but I had no trouble identifying with "Sweet Baby James," James Taylor…"Fire and Rain" as the latterday translation of "O Susanna," by an old (folks at) home neighborhood native…"Where You Lead, I Will Follow," Carole King… "Almost Heaven" and "Put Your Hand In the Hand" and "Share the Land" and most every other single in that spring's air. While I was out, all the music changed[*].]

***

The first major discovery upon my return to 45 Tiemann was the toilet. It had in fact become a terrarium, habitat for a profusion of multicolored colonies of molds, bacteria, algae, and who knows what other flora and fauna, thriving on the stopped-up-solid jumbo bowl of shit.

Above the bathroom tissue roll I had long ago stuck a facsimile of a prop from *2001*:

ZERO GRAVITY TOILET
Instructions for Use.

---

[*] One can miss a lot by being media-deprived. Other novelties: fluffy blow-dried men's hair, doubleknit fabrics, suits with spinnaker-sized lapels, and hot pants, promptly forbidden as office wear per SSCandB memo.

Reality is not funny. Reality stunk. In one breath I dumped in an entire bottle of Lysol Deodorizing Cleaner: "Kills odor-causing germs...Makes your kitchen smell as clean as it looks." However, this was the bathroom, which soon smelled like a blend of shit and Lysol Deodorizing Cleaner. Then I blasted the dungheap with several minutes' worth of Lysol Brand Spray Disinfectant, which not only actually eliminates odors — doesn't just cover them up...it kills household germs — even flu viruses on environmental surfaces. The spray cut the stench but not entirely and not for long. I added half a flask of Mennen Skin Bracer® Wild Moss, which merely superimposed a green puddle on the coprolith, and a lush lawn topnote on the thickening room air.

The clog just sat there, implacable, impenetrable. Finally I found Alex, who took one whiff, one glance, and called Glick the Plumber, who came in minutes and promptly dispatched the whole biohazard to the homey environment of the Hudson.

***

As far as I knew, from then until whenever, insofar as I could be, I was at large, at liberty, *ad libitum*. So I went for walks. (Nat was once asked where I was, and he said "Wiz is taking a walk."

"When do you expect him back?"

"Probably sometime today."

"*Today?*"

"He takes long walks.")

The walks took me places where I never knew there were places before: around the meatpacking houses down in Manhattan Valley...across the Riverside Drive viaduct to the 130s or 140s and down St. Nicholas Avenue...up to the sludge scow pier out over the Hudson...to the countless cubbies and crannies and alleys all over the neighborhood and its neighborhoods...at any hour, in any weather. Wherever I went, it seemed like every time I turned around there was a Tactical Patrol Force wagon with a sergeant at the wheel — always a big sergeant, since TPF cops had to be over six feet, crewcuts optional.

On Claremont Avenue, two guys stopped me because they needed $2 for wine, so they claimed. "Sorry. Hey, all I got is $1 for beer." No sooner had I gone a few doors further on when a short man jumps in front of me and flashes his tin.

153

"Police officer. Those guys give you any trouble?"

"Naw. Said they wanted $2 for wine. I said I had $1 for beer."

The next time I headed to the bodega for beer for me and Swazey, the door was posted by two cops in riot gear, hats and bats.

***

Leaving Riverside Park one afternoon, I met three kids and one lethal length of pipe. "We don't want to hurt you. We just want your money."

"Aww, hell, sorry, gentlemen, but I didn't bring my wallet to the park. Wait. I might have some loose change."

"Shit. Never mind."

A little ways down the path, a lug in a windbreaker, overdressed for the day, pulled up alongside and held out a gold detective's shield. "What was going on with those kids?"

"They said they didn't want to hurt me, just wanted my money. Tall kid had a nice piece of lead pipe, just dangling it, real casual."

"They get anything?"

"I told 'em I didn't take my wallet to the park."

Up on the Drive, I saw that cop and those kids in what seemed to be a serious but one-sided discussion. Around a corner, down a street, there were the kids again, but this time, no pipe.

"Hey, mister, we're sorry. Didn't mean you any trouble."

Lordy. Armed robbers apologizing.

"Don't worry about it. No hard feelings. It's OK. I'll see ya around."

***

In an alley near the cab garages, a car was on fire, "going good," the FD would say. I looked, looked closer, then decided to walk by the fire, which practically meant walking through it, since flames were sticking out across half the sidewalk. I'm fearless. I cannot come to harm. What if the gas tank blows up? Uh-oh. Walk faster. Then an engine company running down Broadway spotted the bonfire, backed up and cruised the wrong way down the street to the car. Nice easy booster tank job.

***

Annapurna invited me to visit her in the Riverside Drive apartment she was house-sitting for Edward Jay Epstein. *The* Edward

154

Jay *Rush to Judgment* Epstein. I got buzzed in readily enough, but a uniformed cop rode all the way up in the elevator with me.

"I've heard of high security buildings, but this is a bit much."

"Wiz, do you know who lives here?"

"Lemme guess. Alexander Kerensky."

"He lived next door. Frank Hogan lives here."

"Frank Hogan the D.A.?"

"Frank Hogan the Manhattan D.A. You saw what happened last night?"

"That was *here?*"

Last night the radio car always posted outside the building got suckered into a moving violation stop and an automatic weapons ambush. The car ended up like a prop from *Bonnie and Clyde*.

***

Gail the illustrator invited me down to the Barnard dorms, to a room that looked like an explosion in the global village cottage industries — all strung and strewn with macramé, batiks, block prints, silk screens, wood and stone totemic figures and other self-made ethnographic artifacts.

(Gail wasn't ethnic, but sure wanted to be. I had always wondered about '60s students' infatuation with primitive and peasant lifestyle and culture. After all, that was what my grandparents had come from the Old Country to escape. Pretending to be folk — not that anybody was fooling anybody — might be entertaining, but the trappings seemed like so much Hallowe'en costumery without the actual life and status. Admiring the working class, not only a Marxist but a liberal principle of faith, seemed at best naive in people who never belonged to that class, especially to those of us who sought the establishment's education, acceptance, and employment to move up out of the proletariat. We knew people who worked for wages every day; we did not want their jobs or their hard hassled lives. Where I came from, work shirts did not pass as play clothes. Condemning materialism, as so many of us did with fervent moral certainty, sounded phony with so much material around. Give me the simple life, but don't take away my camera, my stereo, or my summer in Europe.)

Gail had a portfolio of new work that she wanted me to see — a series of a dozen or so bold watercolors depicting a stylized, allegorical, Edenic drama. A tense, attenuated, Giacomettish figure[*] wandered in and out of a thick and dismal wood. Page by page, she narrated: "Here he is braving the darkness and prevailing through the ordeal. Here he has yielded to his weakness and shame. Then he determines to face the dangers. Now he rises to walk in the light toward his hope...."

Well, well. Was she watching the training too, or did the story come from a pool feed? Unmistakable resemblance or uncanny coincidence.

***

I kept getting invited to dinners: seven straight days hand running, every gracious friend served chicken. Each and every chicken was baked. No fried, no *cacciatore*, nothing but plain, simple, roasters. That *had* to be a conspiracy. I also found food: in the apartment hallways, a full bunch of broccoli, unopened ...an eggplant...a fresh sheaf of asparagus...(mercifully) two pieces of Kentucky Fried Chicken and a roll, still warm...a soupbone, straight from the butcher. Further, found a big, nearly new Zenith AM-FM radio: the old one, tuned to the closed circuit carrier current narrowcasts, seemed to have burned out.

I started shopping at the Food Co-Op off W. 125th Street on the Harlem side of Grant Houses. Not only did it seem like the right thing to do, but they cashed my checks without a hassle[**], and the prices were lower than the Daitch Shopwell around the corner or the A&P down the block. The grocery lists were simple and frugal — originally,

Pullman loaf white bread
1 lb. margarine
1 lb. Kraft® American Singles™

---

[*] Gail had already illustrated me (from visual imagination — I didn't model) in Jockey® shorts, over-the-calf socks, and wingtips for the draft physical story, so she had the proportions down, although I thought the new stylized renditions offered a better likeness, especially since the weak chin didn't show.

[**] With over a grand in checking, and maybe $6k in savings and lump sum profit sharing in the Bowery Savings Bank (chosen for its convenient 42nd Street subway station branch and because I really liked the name), I figured I could subsist indefinitely.

Cafe Bustelo® instant coffee,
and once on impulse,
8-pack Reese's® Peanut Butter Cups.
Remembering the admonition to "keep it kosher," I avoided the issue of *kashruth* pretty much entirely. But discovering that new Kraft Singles included as much polyethylene wrapping as cheese, I switched to
1 lb. Velveeta®.
Calculating that peanut butter cups cost more per ounce than steak, I substituted
Large jar Skippy® Peanut Butter (Chunky Style).
Finally, understanding that kosherish did not mean vegan, I moved up the food chain to
Chicken, cut up, giblets included,
and now and then,
1 lb. ground beef.
To satisfy a craving and make a statement of solidarity or something,
1 lb. Shabazz sausage
In another impulse,
6-pack Cerveza Malta,
thick, semi-sweet non-alcoholic malt beverage often served to Hispanic children. Funny. I wasn't drinking much anymore.

Expanding my tastes further, Leslee fed me matzoh brie, rhubarb pie, artichokes with drawn butter, and more of her secret recipe cannabiscuit chocolate cookies. Kirk and Jan had left a dozen bottles of homebrew, *Lowbrau*, piss yellow atop thick sediment, but not bad, considering. Meantime, Mizz Swazey still brought in the occasional treat, and once even took me to breakfast, down to the Riverside Cafe for a few glasses of their special fortified orange juice. Larry & Co. treated me to a Japanese dinner — a teriyaki, since sushi was not yet trendy — with the obligatory ritualistic hot towels and blood-heat sake. After dinner I realized that I was wearing my red-and-blue-on-white striped tie. Real smart, flying the corporate colors around your neck. Jeez. How obvious can you get? As casually but quickly as I could, I undid the tie and rolled it into a pocket. "Suddenly started to feel real warm out here."

***

Standing at the living room window I lit a cigar. The phone rang. Leslee said she would be in the neighborhood shortly. Aha. "Send up Smoke."

***

Saturday evenings I would go down to the newsstand for a pack of Antonio y Cleopatra Tribunes® small cigars (American Tobacco Client product) to accompany the Sunday *Times* and *Daily News*. The latter I got for the comics, which were curiously, coincidentally funny:

✐ "Smitty," light office-water-cooler-humor strip: "Bailey [the Boss] is a sentimental old coot." Hey. Wow. I wrote that very line about Bayles.

✐ "Dondi," heartwarming adventures of WWII orphan adopted by G.I.: kid's eyes pop as he sees he's going to fly in his own 707. Me too after Christmas.

✐ "Dick Tracy," new villain named "Pouch," who concealed a pistol in his neck wattles. "Wizard," I had been told, "you need a police permit for your voice."

I remember only these offhand, but there were several in each Sunday edition.

***

For a change of scene I would occasionally patrol through Times Square, albeit during afternoons rather than my previous midnight cowboy tours. I felt I really belonged down there: everyone on those streets looked the way I felt. Nights were living theater, cast of thousands, spectacularly realistic sets. Afternoons were just matinees with understudies. Thus on The Deuce — 42nd Street — I frequented the 99¢ double features at the appropriately named Empire Theater: "Patton" and "M*A*S*H," "Dr. No" and "From Russia With Love," and other second-run combos. Every one was a wide-screen full-length series of practical "LOOK BEFORE BACKING" case histories. Even here, as soon as I got settled into a balcony seat, a well-dressed goon came along and stationed himself on the aisle.

Per his request, I had to call Bill Timm about some kind of final technicality or unfinished business formality.

"Morning, sir. This is Jim Wisniewski."

"WHO?"

***

"Hey, chief, how do I get back on the West Side Highway?", fella hollers out of a car on a cobblestone street flanking the waterfront.

"Turn around and go up that way."

"Huh?"

"Make a U-turn. MAKE A U-TURN." I draw a "U" in the air.

Down a ways on the sidewalk, a flurry of taxicab trip sheets, all printed bold,

NO U-TURNS.

***

My inflatable couch made telltale noises, so Swazey must have heard me turn to look at the wall clock.[*] "They hang around. They'll be back," she said. And right there was the answer to the remaining crypto question of "Uncle John's Band" by The Grateful Dead:

Where does the time go?

I already had the answers to the others:

Are you kind?

Have you seen the like?

How does the song go?

Will you come with me?

This was the anthem. "Come hear Uncle John's Band by the riverside/Got some things to talk about, here beside the rising tide." A rising tide lifts all the boats. I knew what my Vonnegutsy wampeter was. And Uncle John is....

***

---

[*] Above the clock, a Prestype-on-shirt-cardboard self-motivational sign, the McDonnell-Douglas DC-10 slogan in its competition with the Lockheed L-1011: **"Fly before they roll."**

Good Friday. On the radio, a devotional service: "Now the baritone Richard Uhl with a selection from Handel" — "The trumpet shall sound and the dead shall be raised incorruptible." (I had often thought of myself as Conrad's *capataz de cargadores*, Nostromo the Incorruptible — except I hadn't figured my price yet.)

Easter Sunday. At sunrise I went to the roof as the Riverside Church carillon rang out over western Manhattan, across the Hudson and back again to the silent city. Then, as personal Paschal tradition, I read from Fitzgerald:

> And as the moon rose higher the inessential houses began to melt away until gradually I became aware of the old island here that flowered once for Dutch sailors' eyes — a fresh green breast of the new world. Its vanished trees, the trees that had made way for Gatsby's house, had once pandered in whispers to the last and greatest of all human dreams — for a transitory enchanted moment man must have held his breath in the presence of this continent, compelled into an aesthetic contemplation he neither understood nor desired, face to face for the last time in history with something commensurate with his capacity for wonder.
>
> Gatsby believed in the green light, the orgiastic future that year by year recedes before us. It eluded us then, but that's no matter — tomorrow we will run faster, stretch out our arms farther... And one fine morning —

Then "the Jesus Prayer" I learned when Leslee had me read *Franny and Zooey*:

> I move not without Thy Knowledge.

***

From right across the street, I watched Lyndon Johnson, Leroi Jones, and John V. Lindsay, among the other honorary pallbearers, come out of Riverside Church at Whitney Young's funeral. Above us all, through the park to the Hudson Valley, the carillon rang "We Shall Overcome." Surprisingly, or maybe not, people were embracing and smiling in that splendid spring midday.

***

I often read aloud — Yeats on St. Patrick's Day, Thomas Wolfe in grandiose moments, Joaquin Miller on Columbus for morale, and two or three times over one day, MacManus, John & Adams's entry in TIME's "Power Of Print" showcase series of *pro bono* ads, with some lines I still recall:

> "I have died in Viet Nam. But I have walked the face of the moon....
>
> "I have built a bomb to destroy the world. But I have used it to light a light....
>
> "I have watched children starve from my golden towers. But I have fed half of the earth....
>
> "I live in the greatest country in the world in the greatest time in history. But I scorn the ground I stand upon.
>
> "I am ashamed. But I am proud.
>
> "I am an American."

Over beer, Swazey began reminiscing about her Canadian bluenose nationality.

"James, didn't you tell me that you were Canadian?"

"No, Mizz Swazey. I am an American." It just came out.

✳✳✳

The Flying Dutchman

Before dawn I found myself at the foot of Manhattan at the Staten Island Ferry terminal. When I went to get change for the nickel fare, the clerk told me, "Go through the island" — the gate between the banks of turnstiles — so I got a free ride.

Not many people headed for Staten Island at this hour. The dock doors opened, we meandered onto the ramps, and I noticed that this was a brand-new bright orange-and-blue[*] boat. Up on the white wooden wheelhouse, the name, which I had never seen before:

AMERICAN
LEGION

As the ferry ground out into the gray hard harbor, I went forward onto the hurricane deck and looked up beyond the bow. Dead ahead there was a police launch leading us.

To save the return fare, in port on Staten Island I squatted down and sidled into the column boarding the Manhattan-bound boat. Could have just as easily stowed away in the head, which had an ad poster right outside:

HN1050. For Traffic Headaches.

Under way, the main deck all full of commuters stayed absolutely silent. No morning chitchat or sports replays or news analysis or shoptalk: *not one word*. Not even a cough or a shuffle of feet or rattle of papers.

The sun rose over Brooklyn. I have never seen such a sun as that morning: a pure solid radiant red perfect sphere hung no higher than

---

[*] Orange for the Dutch, blue for the ocean. "The colors of the City of New York," I declared to Vinnie when he admired my shirt and tie in that combo. (During the Peacock Revolution, one could get away with anything.) "Sanitation Department colors," he sniffed.

the office buildings in back of the Battery. I could not keep myself from looking, gaping, nor my mind from repeating the simple solemn incantation,

Little wheel, spin and spin;
Big wheel turn around and around.

Then — it must have been over the P.A. system — I heard this:

Whatever happens here and whatever you do, we want you to remember one thing every morning over your coffee:

Remember that all things come from the Sun. It rises in the east and sets in the west and it shines on everybody, but it shines on us first. When it goes out, we all go out. So as long as it shines on you, you work for it.

(To this day, over my morning coffee....)

On the bench across from me, a peajacketed man unclasped his hands to reveal a thick gold ring on his right middle finger. The Fair Ring. All's fair in love and war. That's when it's OK to use the middle finger. Never lose sight of the ring.

I got off the boat exultant and reverent and afraid. *Nunc dimittis, Dominum nostrum servum tuum....* Now, o Lord, dismiss Thy servant....

As I looked back, the harbor's deckplate gray had gone to gloss white and blue enamel and mica. Then from the Ferry's auto deck and onto Manhattan came two tractor trailer trucks, dark tinted glass in the conventional cabs, hauling shrouded flatbed-long loads. I had never before seen trucks on the ferry from Staten Island. And never anywhere had I heard truck engines this smooth and quiet, the sound as soft as an electric fan.

***

Signed, sealed, and delivered

"Raid!" shrilled out in the hall. Bug out. Finally. I flung the Sentinel into the floor and stomped on the spilled electronics. Free of that, at least. Then one morning, half awake, I heard through the bedroom wall yet another folky line,

I'll show you a young man with so many reasons why;

There but for fortune go you or I.

And a voiceover: "We just wanted you to know that Tony Schwartz did the sound for all this. Tony Schwartz made those tapes." Hey. Now that's something. I remember meeting Tony Schwartz in his brickhouse 12th Avenue studio. He was best known for the LBJ 1964 "Daisy" spot, but uniquely distinguished for putting the City on record — whole albums and films and libraries of the sounds of New York in all its audible definitive declarations. So that very Tony Schwartz was the one who audio-engineered my adventure — the sound effects that played from outside and the stories in my hypnopaedic dreams. How 'bout that? Nothing but the best.

***

Mr. Henry the Janitor in Ferris Booth Hall got me going once again — this time walking the 73 blocks down to SSCandB and beating the morning rush hour. Just a popin dropby, ostensibly to see that my stuff would finally get shipped uptown, and to deliver to Vinnie a New York attractions coloring book, available only at the gift shop at the top of the Empire State Building, where I went to cross the end of the block on 34th Street.

Funny, but everyone I met was flashing fair rings or pinky rings aimed right at my eyes. Vinnie offered yet another epigram: "Big balls hang low."

Straight out my old office window, the light burned in the same place in the black building, now flanked by an identical tower with a facade made of mirrors, showing off the clouds.

On my way out, I stopped at the newsstand in the lobby to buy a *New York* magazine and a pack of Pall Malls, per regular habitual practice. I had stopped smoking, not missing it in the slightest or even thinking about it. The cigarettes were a statement, here in the home of the brand. You sell 'em, I can buy 'em. Nyah nyah. And surely the Agency would not doctor up its biggest Client's product.

I went down to my private lunchtime thinking place, a tiny walkway out a few yards into the East River, the UN to starboard, Roosevelt Island and the Delacorte Fountain to port, the highway and all of Manhattan astern. I smoked a few of my Pall Malls with overdone obvious drama. Then upriver came an unladen freighter with

NO SMOKING

ruling over the deck, letters painted ten feet high across the superstructure. Most merchant vessels bore such a sign. But down there on the FDR Drive, a "NO SMOKING" sign popped up in the back window of an unmufflered, burnt-oil-blowing taxi. In the park above the highway, a kid hollered "Mommy! Mommy!"

***

The last time I was around Herald Square, I went to the General Post Office to mail some letters. By coincidence I was wearing a stubbly beard, glasses, and an army field jacket — just as my *doppelganger* did that first night when he said in Seeger's voice, "I'LL DE-CON*FUSE* THEM." (Maybe I *did* sound a lot like Pete after all.) The same sign I recalled from that night hung over one of service windows:

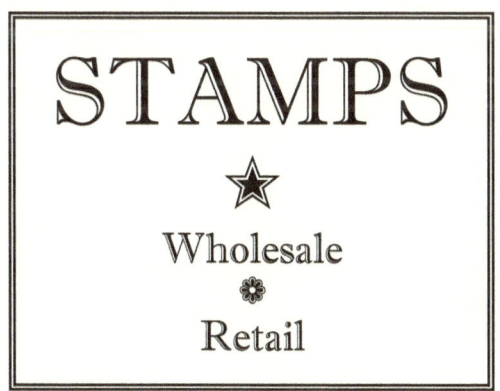

***

Bella the Landlord called, alleging that I had caused the ceiling of the apartment below to collapse.

<<WHA?>>

"Vishnyevskee, you were playing with your duck in your bathtub and made water everywhere."

"It's not a duck, Mrs. Geliebter. It's a frog." In fact, I did have a rubber frog that stuck its tongue out when squeezed. But I did not play with it in the bathtub. For that matter, I took showers, not baths. And Apartment 5F's ceiling was still securely and fully attached to my floor. Gotta be another joke.

Then the City stuck up a paper on the front door —

𝕹otice of 𝕰biction

— citing the frog, the bathtub, the ceiling, two months' rent due, and the delinquent negligent offending party, spelled "Vishnyevskee."

<<WHA?>>

I went to see 45 Tiemann Associates, namely Bella and her rabbi husband. They didn't even want the back rent.

Now I got it. Vacancy decontrol. If a tenant in a rent-controlled apartment died, moved, or was evicted, rent control no longer applied to those premises. $111.91 a month could get hiked to whatever the market and the traffic would bear. Of course they didn't want my rent. Nor me. Thank you, Nelson A. Rockefeller.

Then again, so what? For all I know, this is how I am gonna get moved. So let's get a move on. For all I care, there's nothing much happening here anymore anyway. Enough already. And for what it's worth, this could be just another subplot in a thus far absurd scenario. OK. Carry on. Surprise me.

One morning in late June a tubby city marshal, his movers, and a pair of 2-6 Precinct cops forced entry, no-knock, unannounced, through the safety panel in the front door. <<Must be part of the plan. Go with it.>> The new super, Señor Rubén, came in and offered to hold my penny bank — outsize Welch's Grape Juice can replica — and my ad copy portfolio for safekeeping. In the midst of the moving, I excused myself to take a dump, which I was sitting and doing when a cop barged in.

"Whaddaya doing in here?"

"Taking a dump, officer. Whassit look like?"

The marshal told me I had 60 days to claim my belongings down at 125 Worth Street. Then he said I should leave.

166

"Don't come back here."

"Don't come back here," echoed one of the cops.

I took a small plaid canvas bag of stuff and a dollar and went up to go ride the subways. After a day rattling around I surfaced to crash with Nat Wander and Andy Bronin, who wanted his $2 back from months ago, but they did have a free room and a spare bed.

I slept in a lot. Went for long walks. Checked the listings at the University housing office for a new apartment. Floated the idea of going on welfare. Nat thought that was no way to live. Nor was this. After a few days we got our yakking caught up on, not that I could say much. Nat and Andy had classes and work. I didn't. Not even a TV to watch, little of interest to read. Tuna fish seemed to be the only thing to eat. No beer in the house unless I brought it in, which made me feel dissolute.

* * *

With $5 burning a hole in my pocket, I headed up Broadway past the cab garages to find a bar. Next to a storefront Pentecostal church in full frantic *agape,* I came across a little joint named *Sans Souci*, not coincidentally the title of a traditional Columbia College drinking song.* A Spanish bar — (What did I expect up here? A preppy post-grad club?) — but being the only Anglo in the place didn't bother me. I ordered a vodka martini. Then the jukebox played "Uncle John's Band." Twice. I ordered two or three more vodka martians and went back to Nat's place, clenching my teeth and squinting my eyes as every feeling I knew I could have just ran through me and broke in out-of-phase waves.

* * *

My welcome and I were wearing out. Nat cast my I Ching, which seemed to point me to Jackson Hole, Wyoming, although the description fit Pittsburgh just as well. On the bus back, I half expected Philadelphia to light up for me.

* * *

---

* "What if tomorrow bring sorrow or anything other than joy?
What if't be wintry chill, rain, storm, or summer's thrill?
Tomorrow's the future still. This is today!"
And so forth, *sans souci*, as per directions. *Carpe* Ngo Dinh Diem. *Lumpen*throat. Other songs, such as "The Freshmen Up At Yale (Get No Tail)" and "Raw, Eat It Raw" (a parody of "Roar, Lion, Roar") are in bad taste at best.

167

OCCUPANT

"If you're going to stay here you'll live by our rules." The Old Man laid down the law.

I was 23 years old and I needed rules. Perhaps so: these were special, customized, personalized, *ad hoc* rules. In summary:

§ Whatever you do is against the rules.

In principle:

§ You were not particularly welcome here in the first place. In conclusion:

§ If you don't like it, leave.

In practice, I was ostracized — not to mention browbeaten, cursed, insulted, threatened, shaken, pushed, kicked, routinely slandered, categorically blamed, and frequently denied basic needs from food to laundry. But what did I expect? I was yet another open leprous sore spot causing familial embarrassment. First my brother the junkie, now me, the dropout unemployed hippie mental case. Sorry, but not that I had much of anyplace else to go. Nor, if that's what the Old Man intended, was the treatment going to get rid of me. Not likely, not after what I had been through.

***

Nobody once asked what happened. No one. Not once. Not that I could have disclosed much nor detailed anything. But I was never asked what went wrong at work. Or what went on over those months. Nor what my diagnosis was down at Bellevue, nor my treatment, nor prognosis nor followup. Not even "How are you doing now? Are you OK? Can we help?"

Not that this sort of thing would be discussed anyway. Nor that I actually expected any expression of concern or extension of support. We just did not behave that way. The eastern European ethnic value system stressed self-reliance and abject stoicism. If you had a problem, it was *your* problem. You take care of it.

People should mind their own business. No one will offer to help, and you should not ask for help. People have problems. Big deal. So what? Get used to it. Live with it. Never flinch. Show nothing. Offer nothing. Reveal nothing. Expressing emotion is manifesting weakness.

Whatever the conditions, regardless of your reactions, under all circumstances, maintain the dead pan. As Nat Wander once remarked, "Wizard, I've seen you when I know you've been deliriously happy, and when I know you are despondently sad, and you look the same. No change. No difference."

All this came straight from the top down. The ethnic god was fearsome and just: the reason for leading a good life, by the letter of the law, was to avoid punishment. Rather than hoping for mercy, one fretted about getting nailed on a technicality. Instead of growing in love, one obeyed in lockstep. Life was a test, trial by ordeal, and you were on your own. "So help me God" was an oath, not a prayer.

***

"Mark, did anyone give my father the whole story about what happened? Any idea what he was told?" No help.

"Hey, Vinnie, what's goin' on there? Anything happening I oughta know about?" No help there either.

"Hiya Judy. You remember the last time we talked and you told me I had good grades....?"

Strike three. OK. I tried. Now it's on them.

***

I never gave up hope. Every day could be it. "We'll be by to pick up our prize package after lunch." 2:30 in the afternoon, any day now.

After months I had less to hold onto, holding tighter. They'll come when I least expect it. Or on some significant day when I should have expected them all along. All along, I saw them coming — in a car with rear window backup lights, in a swarm of postal vehicles, or just one red-white-and-blue special delivery station wagon at a propitious time and place. I heard them in Muzak, read them in graffiti, felt them walking behind me, just around the corner. I sought them in memory, down all the steps of every incident, in playback, analysis, exegesis, rewind and replay of each line, word, inflection, punctuation. I found them finding me only in two glorious dreams, which I knew were only wishful.

***

Bus back to New York to retrieve the stuff evicted from the apartment. "Great is the power of the city to call the wanderer home" — O. Henry.

169

The City office could not find a record of the property. Then it occurred to me that the file would be under "Vishnyevskee," not "Wisniewski." The clerk turned surlier.

"Why didn't you tell me that *in the first place*?"

"I filled out the card with my right name. I showed you my I.D."

"You can't use two different names."

"I don't. The landlord used one. That's not how my real name is spelled."

The clerk found the file under "VISHNYEVSKEE." "This doesn't match the name on your I.D. This isn't your property."

"It certainly is my property. It came from my apartment."

"But the name on the file is 'VISHNYEVSKEE.' *You're* not that *person*."

"The landlord spelled my name phonetically."

"What?"

"Spelled it the way it sounds in Polish."

"Why isn't it in English?"

"She spelled it according to the way it's pronounced — in Polish. She's one of the few people I know who can pronounce it right. I think she's originally from eastern Europe somewhere, Latvia or Russia or thereabouts, so she knows how it's supposed to sound."

"It doesn't *matter* how it sounds. I don't *care* how it sounds. It's what's on the *paper*. VISHNYEVSKEE...WISNIEWSKI: those are two different names."

"Same name, just English or Polish."

"This isn't *Poland*. This is New York. This should be in English.*"

"It is in English. No, it isn't. Wait. Can I explain this? See, here's how it sounds. W-I-S-N-I- E-W- S-K-I... Vish-NYEV-skee. Same thing. See, a 'W' in English is pronounced as a 'V' in Polish. The 's' has an 'sh' sound. So, 'VISH.' The 'ni' comes out like 'ny,'

---

* I refrained from mentioning that the maternal side of the family, Dutch, was here before both the English and the Republic. A delicate subject, since they seem to have been in the human resources import business. Further, they produced my multi-great grandfather, among the least distinguished presidents of the United States, one Martin van Buren. Only relative ever portrayed in the movies, most unfavorably but I guess accurately by Spielberg in "Amistad."

and the next 'w' is a 'v,' like before, so together, it's "VISHNYEV...."

Ellis Island all over again. Finally the clerk relented and stamped the umplicate forms authorizing release of the property from the Bronx Encumbrance Depot.

Encumbrance. Jeez.

***

"It's a long story...."

That's typically how I've had to explain what happened, and why and how I ended up here. Not that it says much of anything, not that I very well could. But here we are. In short, for the record:

§ Young & Rubicam was awarded the original Postal Service account, and has retained it ever since, doing admirable work.

§ Apollo XIV and subsequent missions applied obscure, mythological or commonplace names to their vehicles.

§ The Belgian blocks that inspired the naming of Sesame Street were asphalted over in the summer of 1971. ("They paved Paradise, put up a parking lot." — Joni Mitchell.)

§ The North American Van Lines agent had me come down to their warehouse to verify that the stuff they picked up in the Bronx was indeed my stuff. "This is the worst shipment I've ever seen," said the agent. Yeah, well, the city marshal may not share your standards of customer service. At least the clothes are in a couple of refrigerator-size boxes. And I naturally expected the radio to be pilfered. But a wall's worth of books? Worst of all, Sr. Rubén the Super didn't remember anything at all about the portfolio he offered to hold in safekeeping for me. *"No me recuerdo,"* followed by the *"No me entiende"* defense, except that *yo se hablo Spanglish sin acénto.* Shit. Standing rule among copywriters and art directors: in case of fire, flood, or nudet, save the portfolio first. Then rescue the kids and the dog. The penny hoard, no loss. I hope it went to a good cause.

§ The newest resident I know of at 45 Tiemann Place, #6F, was a baby christened Elvis Napoleon, last name unknown, but with those first two, who needs one?

§ S. Heagan Bayles died at age 85 in February, 1996.

§ The Old Man died at age 54[1] in March, 1973.

§ As a consequence, I became legal guardian[2] of my sister[3], then 15. After high school, she joined the U.S. Marine Corps[4], subsequently got a Master's in Social Work[5], and currently serves as a therapist working with sex offenders. Go figure.

§ My brother died at age 37[6] in May, 1988.

§ For some time, I kept in fairly close contact with some of the principals in this story, but as invariably happens, we lost touch. Meantime, even in response to direct questions, nobody recalled, much less admitted, any role whatsoever in these incidents. ("I don't remember anything out of the ordinary." "I'm not sure I know what you're referring to." "Wiz, you just dropped out of sight." "Only thing unusual was you flipping out.")

§ SSCandB moved to One Dag Hammarskjold Plaza, became SSCandB/LINTAS, which became LINTAS, which became one of the Interpublic Group of Companies.

§ I retired from advertising in Pittsburgh[7] in 1991, at age 43, and am doing quite nicely[8], thank you very much. But every day I miss the city.

---

[1] Massive coronary occlusion. All I knew how to do was get the O_2 tank out of his office, strap on the mask, compress the chest, and call the cops. By the time the paddy wagon/ambulance arrived with a first aid kit and a pipe stretcher (this was pre-EMS and MICU), he had gone out. En route to the ER, the officers radioed in "Possible DOA," which meant that the entire scanner-intensive neighborhood got the scoop. Later the cops politely expressed regret that it was too late for them to help, assuring me that they did not suspect foul play. Thanks, officers. At the hospital's suggestion, I agreed to an autopsy; then the family doc/family friend called the ER and said it wasn't needed. Who knows? To add just a little more paranoia: the Old Man's last meal was a takeout from the neighborhood greasy spoon. Ultimately, it was going to be him or me, and my position was tenuous.

[2] By sheer default, as the only responsible consenting adult available.

[3] Who once sent me a cartoon: "For years, growing up, I was afraid that maybe I was adopted. Now that I see this family, I'm worried that maybe I wasn't."

[4] Uncle Sam's Misguided Children: CPL, FMFLANT, Norfolk, in Marine Intelligence, which she described as an oxymoron, although not in that exact word.

[5] Editing her sex papers was a revelation. And I thought *I* had a few kinks.

[6]Esophageal varices due to chronic (>20 yrs.) drug and alcohol abuse. No surprise: exhausted predicted nine lives many times over. Survived by former common-law wife, wife, and daughter. Kicked hell out of average immediate family life expectancy.

[7] Having worked for small, medium, and large shops ranging from grossly incompetent to as good as they get. But it's *Pittsburgh*. Industrial accounts, obscure products. Parity (sometimes spelled "parody") commodities, boilerplate strategies. Products that do not respond to advertising, client service that depends on playing golf. Ad managers with half-million dollar budgets who act like Little Caesars. Hardhat-and-safety-goggles plant tours. Small town. Everybody knows everybody else in the business. '50s holdovers. Mediocrities with sportcoats and sinecures. Two or three of the dumbest people I have ever met in business, and two or three of the smartest. Hack shops. Zero-base quality standards. Awful English. Gray suits. Conceptual challenges, technical tedium. Smokestack basic industry, leading edge R&D. Product data sheets. Sales training slide shows. Stock photos. Local talent. UHF-TV station videotape production values. Cornball retail. Canned jingles. Derivative concepts. Devout "Saturday Night Live" fans. Hipper-than-thou creative people who really believe they're creating. Pretension, posturing. Agency people trying real hard to do it the way they imagine it's done in New York, and not quite ever getting it. Overall, *infra dig.* "It's raining, and I'm in Pittsburgh" — Gleason, "Requiem for a Heavyweight."

[8] Confirmed bachelor, but straight, dammit, straight. Ascetic/student lifestyle. Living in a fine 100-year-old (Dakota vintage — same bumps on the walls) highrise apartment building with original oak parquet floors and classical Muzak even in the laundry room. Sober 21 years, major depression successfully treated for 17 years. Cholesterol 161 mg/dl. No communicable diseases. Weight proportionate to height. No police record. Professional, personal, financial references on request.

*** *** ***

A likely story

All this would probably go down a lot easier if I declared that I had been snatched by aliens.

Or I could attribute the events to an ill-conceived but well-concealed operation by COINTELPRO...or CIA MK Ultra...the Nixon White House Plumbers*... psywarriors, military or civilian...the National Security Council (I would rule out the NSA and NRO)...or, for that matter, the Trilateral Commission, INTERPOL, the Church of Scientology, SMERSH, or SPECTRE. After all, conspiracy resonated with the '60s *Zeitgeist*. Paranoia rattled loudly, left and right. Back then we all looked hard over both shoulders and under the mattress. Who knew what evil lurked...?

C'mon. Who's kidding who here? All those sinister powers had bigger fish to filet. I can't imagine fitting anyone's profile or experimental protocol.

How could I miss the most immediate and obvious of the dark forces — the advertising business? The hidden persuaders, subliminal seducers, mind-altering mass movers? An agency could have indeed staged the show — that's what we're supposed to be good at — with a lot of help and a big budget. Not a sound investment, given the target audience. Why spend over six months and well into (estimated/scientific-wild-ass-guess) six figures on an $11,000-a-year, 22-year-old copywriter? Even for a $17 million account, big bucks at the time, worth 10 times more now, that would be pissing away the first potential profits on sheer speculation in advance. Really, now. A B-52 can kill a mosquito, but not cost-effectively.

If the objective was to establish my *bona fides,* that could be accomplished by reviewing my records — SAT scores, the Minnesota Multiphasic Personality Inventory, which I had to take upon entering Columbia, transcripts, tax returns, dental charts, upper and lower G.I. X-rays, employee file, whatever. Also, feel free to interrogate any known associates, using sodium pentathol and scopolamine if desired. Hey, they'd like that. I would have willingly

---

* Actually met G. Gordon Liddy once, in a hardware store in Caldwell, NJ, where he was visiting his Mom and helping out with some repairs around the house. Impressive gent. Scary, too.

signed a loyalty oath and submitted to a polygraph. A drug test might have turned out positive, but that would only prove that I lived in the '60s, when drug tests were fortunately not routinely administered anyway.

I could just call the whole thing a novel and get away with it. That has been suggested: change the names, graft on a dramatic or enigmatic ending, pass it off as a creative work. Recast it as one of those Jay McInerney or Bret Easton Ellis city lifestyle sagas, although even I could not conjure up being chased by a park bench *à la American Psycho*.

Fictionally, I could give you a neatly satisfying ending. For instance:

a) **Going postal.** Not that I didn't fantasize about actually doing that. Variation: pulling a Kaczynski[*]. Not only letter bombs but — aha! — book bombs. Turn this page at your own risk.

b) **Staying crazy.** Bellevue II, this time for real, for good. Raving, up and out.

c) **Losing,** and ending up writing this account in a homeless shelter, where I am in good company, and the story is tame by comparison.

d) **Losing badly** — equivalent to the above, with atrocities thrown in.

e) **Losing but recovering** gracefully, thence writing this but changing all the names and circumstances so as not to jeopardize my position as Creative Director, Worldwide, SSCandB/LINTAS.

f) **Winning.** What an imaginative twist. What a letdown. No story there.

g) **Winning big,** as in the "Miracle on 34th Street" ending, plus lunch with Richard Nixon, key to the city from John Lindsay, ticker tape parade. Sure. Maybe for that would work for "*Long Story*! A New Musical."

h) **Prophesying and pontificating** — the narrative as allegory, the modern urban parable as timeless truth, whether humanist, objectivist, Marxist, existentialist, sado-masochist, or what have you. What this really means is....

---

[*] Pronounced 'ka-CHEEN-skee,' as in Stanley B., M.D., the old neighborhood G.P.

i) **Discovering** that none of these places or people ever existed. The shop, a see-through building. Sesame Street, a parking garage. Park Avenue and the General Post Office would still be landmarks. The people…who? No one by that name. Return to **b)**.

j) **Awakening,** although not sure to what. Naah. Been done.

k) **Emerging** from this adventure only to enter another, even stranger, thus setting up at least a trilogy and perhaps a continuing series.

Choose any or all of the above, or any combination or permutation. Confabulation could be fun. Also dishonest — to the reader, the writer, the story.

If I want to maintain that it happened, so I've been told, admit what *really* happened. Recognize it — and write about it — as what it was: a psychotic break. That diagnosis came unaided, unprompted, and independently among a few people to whom I have related all or part of the story.

I'm looking for an answer, so their analyses demand consideration. For instance, from Alison R. Parker, classicist and newspaper copy editor:

….it almost seems, at times, that you have spent the past quarter-century constructing a religion to yourself, complete with *mysterium fidei*, as you put it: a (Grateful Dead) hymn, a festival (Macy's Thanksgiving Parade), at least one commandment that you use over and over (Look before backing), a temple (NY post office), and a sort of holy bible, albeit in a most 20th-century medium ("Miracle on 34th Street.")….

Thence the obvious question: "Why does it upset you so much that people tend to believe it a psychotic break? Is there shame in that?"

If it were a psychotic break, I would readily admit to it. I've admitted to worse. I have nothing to hide. No stigma.

And, as my sister the M.S.W. noted, a psychotic break ends. "I was away for a little while. Now I'm back. I feel much better now."

After nearly 30 years, I'm still away, out there. To me, here, the incidents and images persist clearly, consistently, as undeniable (to me) actual direct personal experience. I still maintain, as then and forevermore, that *this happened.* Understanding at least the obvious differences between reality and illusion, reason and irrationality, vision and hallucination, fact and fable, I *know* all of this to be true.

I also realize that it is unbelievable. There's the catch. Gotcha. The very implausibility enables plausible deniability. If it sounds too unusual to be true, then of course it's untrue. Besides, consider the source. I am an escaped mental patient. *You* try to live that down. *You* try to be taken seriously.

<< "*Gulag*? What *gulag*? How can you listen to that wacko Solzhenitsyn? He's crazy. It's all in his head.">>

<< "House arrest? Internal exile? Sakharov! What an imagination! There is that fine line between genius and madness.">>

<< "How melodramatic. FBI surveillance. Bugs. J. Edgar's secret files. Really, now.">>

<<"A beautiful mind!">>

OK, so prove it. Gimme a break. I don't know how. I am not an investigative journalist, nor is this an exposé. As if those responsible would leave proof lying around for "60 Minutes," the General Accounting Office, congressional committees, federal grand juries, or a Freedom of Information Act request. As if they left *me* with any probative evidence. Like I would testify anyway. I appreciated the meaning of *omertá.* Cross your block and a building falls on you.

For all I know, soon after this sees print, the fit hits the shan.[*] Can't wait.

OK, so prove that it *wasn't* a psychotic break. But that's an attempt to prove a negative.

I can speculate my way into presumption and pridefulness. If anything, I would like to believe in something like the Guardians from Eliot's *The Cocktail Party.* Perhaps it was people like these who selected, protected, trained and tested me. But to what end? For what mission? And when? And what makes me so goddamn special anyway?

"Go, and work out your salvation with diligence." I'm trying. I'm trying.

---

[*] Just coincidentally: first time I tried to send this manuscript to the publisher, via postpaid, pre-addressed Priority Mail with return address, it never got there. Uh-oh.

On the Judeo side of the spectrum, in the ultra-orthodox range, from a Lubavitcher friend — according to Chasidic tradition, there are always thiry-six just men, the *Lamed-Vov*, whose existence, unbeknownst to themselves, justifies humankind to the Lord, and without whom the earth would be shattered. Even ecumenically, something of a denominational stretch for me, and geographically a redundancy, since we seem to have a reputed *Lamed-Vovnik* in the neighborhood, a *tzaddik* readily recognizable in behaviors that might be construed as schizophrenia in a mere mortal. Which is all I claim or aspire to be anyway. No charism here.

Besides, as Thomas Merton noted, God is not a magician. Everything that happened was feasibly human — therefore, by definition, *not* a miracle.

To me, the simplest explanation is that it was what it seemed to be to me.

I know that's an open and unsatisfying ending — unsatisfying especially to me — but until something better comes along, it's the only one I've got.

All I have is my recollection. All you have is my word for it.

Gotta admit, though, at the very least: a lot of strange coincidences.

***

"Thousands at His bidding speed
and post o'er land and ocean without rest.
They also serve who only stand and wait."

For years I expected deliverance. On many occasions I thought, imagined, wished, that "they" were out "there."

Of course they are.

And they know it.

They know exactly what I mean. They know what happened as well as I do. And better.

Having written this, I do not know much more about why this happened. But now I am surer than ever that it *did* in fact happen the way I just told it.

Here is what I do not understand. Three things:

First, what for? To what end? Why such a qualification and indoctrination process, if that's what it was, which it likely wasn't. If not that, what?

I also find it hard to accept that this happened just once, just to this one person. The whole production was too elaborate, too expensive, too smoothly, systematically, effectively executed to have run for just one performance. Was this even the premiere, or a long-run revival? There may well be other people out there who share the same story, not that they could tell it, maybe not until now.

Second, who and how? I can figure out how the buildings lit up, the trains ran, the people marched, the radio played. But specifically, how did so many people, including those I would least expect and most trust, come to be involved? Agency and other employees are easy to explain. They were doing their jobs. They got paid.

I have no idea what motivated everyone else. They couldn't have seen the big picture or the subjective camera view I got. I have no way of knowing who knew how much. I'd like to think that it was strictly need-to-know and largely creative disinformation. How could they *wittingly* have been a part of this? Didn't intelligent, inquisitive, above all independent people at least ask a few fundamental questions?

I'd hate to think that anyone knowingly sold me out. In fact, I can't conceive of it — not these folks, not in that time, not for money, not for power, not for security, not for selfishness. Then for what?

Finally, what did I miss? What did I do or fail to do? What went wrong — and how? What went over my head or fell through the cracks? If I knew that, then possibly I would begin to understand everything else.

One more thing. Now that I have written it all down — now what?

***

For what it's worth — and worth every dime and day invested — I did learn a lot. I figure that I got a full scholarship, room, board, and tuition-paid mail-order degree — a dear school, but an invaluable education. If nothing else, I learned, among other things, that

¶ I've been rich and I've been poor, and poor ain't so bad. In fact, I think it was more peaceful.

¶ I can endure more than I would have ever imagined — not out of sheer resolve or summoned-up strength, but by enduring. Nothing to it but to do it, since there is no alternative. "Life is hard." "Compared to what?"

¶ If this has done nothing else, it has made me more of a patriot than before.

¶ I can still trust anyone until they give me a reason not to. Then, *falsus in unus, falsus in omnibus.*

¶ Incidents and coincidences are different and distinct events, but damned if I know which is which anymore.

¶ There are more powers in heaven and on earth, or at least in New York City, than are dreamt of in your philosophy.

¶ Dropping out of school was the best move I ever made. If I hadn't, I would have missed all this, but of course never would have known what I was missing.

¶ If I had it to do all over again, I would have done it in pretty much the same way.

***

I cannot take any credit for the story. All I did was show up and go where it took me. It happened. I did not plan or plot it. I did not seek it. I did not deserve it, for good or for ill.

No grudges. No recriminations. Everyone was civil. I was not maltreated. No payback. No vindication, not that it matters much anymore. In the long run, on balance, no loss.

My only real regret is that there will be no more miracles. Nothing — but nothing — can follow an act like this. But that is also my greatest gain here, which has kept me going for the past thirty years — mine alone, exclusively, enduringly, uniquely, personally, made-to-order, one-of-a-kind — the unmatched peak experience of a lifetime. Thank you for the story.

By the way, don't say I didn't warn you about the nightmares.

***

—Pittsburgh, Pennsylvania
October, 2002

About the Author

James Casimir Wisniewski, of Pittsburgh, PA, attended Columbia College, New York City, where he majored in English and sociology, served as Editor-without-Diddleywork and Sole Pole, *Jester* humor magazine; literary editor, *COLUMBIAN* yearbook; awarded the James Guttman Prize in the Humanities, elected to the Senior Society of 1848. At 19, he became the youngest copywriter in the business at a major consumer ad agency in New York. After award-winning work at several shops as copywriter, copy chief, and creative director, Wisniewski retired from advertising at age 43, but does not gloat about it.